One Bucket at a Time

Presentation secrets to inform, educate, influence and persuade

Eric Bergman

ISBN: 978-0-9950202-1-4

Table of Contents

"The central theme of this book that a presentation should be a conversation is ingenious. Humans have evolved for hundreds of thousands of years to communicate by conversation. We are mentally structured to do so.

"For anyone seeking to set themselves and their ideas apart, this book is well worth the read. Eric Bergman's techniques are a window to the future of this important human activity."

John Sweller, PhD
Emeritus Professor of Education
University of New South Wales,
Sydney, Australia

PRIME THE PUMP

There was a time, not that long ago, when every medical professional on the planet believed that ulcers were caused by spicy food or stress. In the 1970s, while in my teens, I was diagnosed with a duodenum ulcer. My physician told me it was likely caused by stress. (We knew it wasn't spicy food; my mother, who prepared the vast majority of our meals, was British.) We simply assumed that the environment within the family—my parents were breaking up and it was a few years before they formally split—was the cause.

But now we know better.

In 1982, Drs. Barry Marshall and Robin Warren made the breakthrough discovery that the *H. Pylori* bacterium causes ulcers, for which they were awarded the Nobel Prize in 2005. Between 1982 and today, every physician on the planet has become aware that spicy food and stress do not cause ulcers. But it wasn't easy to get there. For years, Dr. Warren tried to convince his peers that bacteria was the cause, presenting his findings in all the traditional ways. It wasn't until he infected himself with the bacterium to give himself an ulcer that his peers let go of their assumption. But there are still millions of people around the world who believe that spice or stress is the cause. The chances are good that you did until just now.

So what do ulcers have to do with presentations?

My premise is that a large group of highly intelligent, well-educated professionals can fall into a pattern in which they follow a fundamentally incorrect assumption. And they can be incredibly reluctant to let go of that assumption. What was true for ulcers is now true for presentations. Millions of people around the world now believe that showing slides while talking improves communication. We will closely examine that fundamental assumption.

When visual presentation technology emerged, first as 35-mm slides and then overhead acetates, everyone assumed that using visual technology to communicate was better than the alternative of simply talking to people. Nobody challenged that assumption. By the time PowerPoint presentations hit their stride in the 1990s, the assumption was deeply embedded. It wasn't formally tested by cognitive scientists until 2012, twenty-five years after the introduction of PowerPoint. Today, millions of people operate under the fundamental assumption that slides are necessary for presentations. They're not.

The only reason for bringing people together, whether in person or remotely, is to listen to someone share something of value. If there is no speaker, lecturer or presenter, there can be no speech, lecture or presentation. At its core, therefore, presentation effectiveness can be measured by what makes it from the speaker's vocal cords to the long-term memory of those in attendance.

Let's imagine two identical presentations are delivered to two separate audiences. One shows slides, similar to what you've seen thousands of times in your academic and working life. The other doesn't show a single slide to the audience, but delivers the same information verbally and uses a whiteboard or flip chart to explain essential visual concepts. If each audience completes an identical quiz based solely on information from the presentation, which scores higher?

The research is clear. The audience that didn't see slides scores twenty to thirty per cent higher on the quiz than those who attended the slide presentation.

We have moved away from presentations as conversations and, for the sake of communication effectiveness, we need to move back. This book is designed to help you do exactly that. The information here will help make any presentation you deliver more meaningful and memorable.

It is absolutely possible for a large group of highly intelligent people to follow an incorrect assumption, despite the best intentions of everyone involved. The physician who treated my ulcer didn't deliberately give me bad advice. He provided his best advice, but it was based on an incorrect assumption.

If you give the ideas here a chance, they will improve your communication effectiveness. They will help you get more of what you say into the long-term memory of those who are listening.

The secret to success is simple. Bring meaningful content. Deliver that content in a memorable way. If you do, you significantly increase your chances of informing, educating, influencing or persuading anyone.

FROM TANK TO BUCKET TO TROUGH

You are scheduled to deliver a presentation. You may have delivered thousands, or this may be your first. It doesn't matter. Once you're scheduled to speak to an audience, you have a choice.

You can develop a standard presentation, which you will deliver one slide at a time. Or you can develop a conversational presentation, which you will deliver one idea at a time.

What's the difference? As we'll examine, the differences are significant. But the next time you're at a presentation, look around. (Or, the next time you're attending a presentation online, monitor your own behaviour.) Ask yourself one question: Is the audience (am I) leaning in to listen, or are we tuning out to text?

If the audience is leaning in, they're engaged. If they're engaged, the presentation has a chance at success. If they're texting, e-mailing or preparing a document for their boss with the presentation droning on in the background, they're disengaged. At best, they're barely listening, and that's only if they're motivated to pay any attention at all. If the audience is not listening, how can the presentation be successful? Nobody's listening.

Let's be clear. What the speaker says during a presentation is the only place from which value can and should be found in this unique medium of communication. It doesn't matter whether the presentation is online or in person. It doesn't matter whether it is a project update, a new business pitch, a lecture to undergraduates, an employee information session, a conference presentation, a webinar or a keynote address to thousands. The whole reason for bringing people together is to listen to someone share something of value, ideally in a back-and-forth exchange from which both sides benefit. If the audience is reading, writing, texting, looking at slides, scanning their social media feed, sending an e-mail or reading a document, they cannot be listening. And, ultimately, if they're not listening, what on earth is the point?

According to some estimates when the world locked down for COVID-19, standard presentations were being delivered one slide at a time thirty to forty million times a day around the world. Now they're delivered online. The reality is that most of them consistently overload working memory, which is something we'll carefully examine. And, with working memory in overload, standard presentations are boring to watch and a chore to attend, regardless of whether they're delivered in the room or via Zoom.

According to research conducted by a company in the business of making slides, one-fifth of us would rather visit the dentist than attend a standard presentation. A second fifth would rather do our taxes. A third fifth would rather work on Saturday. And fully one-quarter of us would forego sex tonight. In total, nearly eighty-three per cent of us would rather do something distasteful or forego something pleasurable than attend another standard presentation, delivered one slide at a time.

P erhaps it's worth taking a step back to briefly review the evolution of slides during the past forty years. In 1981, during my last year of college, I worked an internship at a corporation that was preparing a series of employee meetings. The purpose was to inform employees of a shift in strategic direction for the organization, which coincided with a major economic downturn. The presentations were delivered by members of the senior management team at meetings in a variety of geographic locations. Each executive delivered a number of presentations. The year I arrived was the first in which senior executives used 35-mm slides to support their talks.

I spent hours putting slides upside-down into carousels, double-checking each to ensure that the slides were in proper order and identical. At the time, each slide cost seventy-five dollars to produce. There were six carousels, each with about thirty slides. The total cost, with shipping, was about fourteen thousand dollars—a significant sum by today's standards. Forty years ago, it was a staggering amount to spend.

For the next eight to ten years, 35-mm slides cost anywhere from thirty-five to seventy-five dollars each on the open market—to get from designer to computer screen through film processing to audience. They were called "speaker support slides" because that's what they did. They supported the speaker.

PowerPoint was created by Apple as a Macintosh program in 1987 to mimic the horizontal format of 35-mm slides. I actually had the first edition on PowerPoint on my black-and-white Macintosh Plus. Steve Jobs sold the program to Microsoft a few years later. Since then, we've seen Cricket Presents and SlideRocket come and go. Today, we have PowerPoint, Keynote, Prezi, Haiku Deck, Google Slides and others. For our purposes, regardless of the product name (unless it's actually part of a story), we'll simply call it slideware. I've seen them all in action. And they have one thing in common: they overload working memory, making listening to what the presenter is saying as the slides are shown more difficult and reducing what makes it to the collective long-term memory of those in attendance.

Before PowerPoint was introduced in 1987, people always finished the content of their presentations before a single slide was created. They had to; changes were both time consuming and expensive. Today, slideware is used to develop content, leading to the inevitable outcome of too many slides with too much on each.

Every day, presentations are delivered to audiences around the world one slide at a time. The good news is that we have time to catch up on email or plan our next vacation. The bad news is that we now have a new phrase in our vernacular: Death by PowerPoint.

And it's killing our ability to communicate effectively.

W e only have two ways to communicate as human beings. We have the written word and we have the spoken word. Nothing more; nothing less. We can write ideas down for others to read. Or we can verbally share ideas with others. Each form of communication is significantly different; each has its strengths and weaknesses.

The written word captures ideas in space and time. This creates knowledge, which can be built upon and expanded by subsequent generations. The written word is great for transferring large amounts of data. I once had a conversation with an accountant who believes you can examine a company's general ledger, which lists every transaction the organization enters into, and rebuild every one of the thousands of decisions made during any period in question. The data of those thousands of decisions are captured in transactions. The transactions are captured in writing.

The spoken word is horrible for transferring data (ever played the broken telephone game?) but is fantastic for putting ideas into perspective. At an effectively run meeting, ideas can be put forward, examined, supported and questioned quickly and efficiently.

One good way to highlight how the written word and spoken word differ is to think of the last time you had an email or text exchange with someone that was going nowhere until you picked up the telephone to chat. Through a back-and-forth discussion, you quickly came to a common understanding. We've all experienced situations like this in which there was value in switching from the written to the spoken word to put ideas into perspective.

Written and oral communication are different. Each has its strengths and weaknesses. But the research is one hundred per cent clear. They work best when they're kept apart.

Reading while attempting to listen doesn't work and should be avoided, regardless of whether you're talking to someone or listening to someone. If I'm talking to my son and he drops his head to read his texts, I stop talking. He's not listening anyway. Likewise, if I'm reading while he's talking, I have to stop reading if I'm interested in what he has to say. If I don't, I won't hear a word. If I try listen while reading, I get nothing from either. Working memory is overloaded.

The fact that working memory is overloaded when we attempt to read and listen at the same time is actually quite easy to test. The next time you're watching your favourite all-news channel, try listening to what the announcer is saying while reading what's scrolling across the screen. Even if both are based on the same story, it shouldn't take more than a few seconds to realize that if you hope to get anything out of the exercise, you have to block out one or the other.

If the audience can understand a presentation by reading the slides (which is, interestingly, one of the flawed reasons for using slides in the first place), why would they listen when those slides are presented? They don't for two reasons. They needn't listen when they can read later, or they simply cannot listen while attempting to read as the presenter is talking.

I once had a discussion with someone who was frustrated because people weren't paying attention during presentations on project updates. The slides for each update were sent in advance. When presenters stood at the front of the room to deliver their presentations, everyone turned to their smartphones and laptops, ignoring the presenter.

"Why are you surprised that nobody's listening?" I asked, after looking at the slides, which were packed with paragraphs and bullet points. "If they've read the slides, they've updated themselves. Since they've already read, and they can read faster than someone else can talk, why would they listen?"

Of course, it could be argued that they could ignore the slides and listen. But if that's the case, why show the slides at all? Why not read the slides, have a brief discussion and answer questions?

That is what LinkedIn has done as an organization, with extremely positive results. The presentation, as a written document in a horizontal slide format (the ubiquitous presentation "deck"), is sent at least twenty-four hours prior to the meeting. If participants haven't read the document, the meeting is stopped and they are given time to catch up. Everyone who has read the document can do something else. When the group is ready, written information is set aside and discussion begins.

The slides are never presented to the group. Instead, the focus is on discussion, a process that distinctly separates the written word from the spoken. LinkedIn has been pleasantly surprised to discover that meetings scheduled for an hour are often completed in twenty to thirty minutes. Decisions are made much more quickly and the decisions themselves are more effective.

Amazon has taken this a step further. They not only separated the written word from the spoken by eliminating slideware presentations at meetings, they also eliminated the transfer of written information via the horizontal presentation deck.

All of their meetings are structured around six-page memos written in a vertical format on a word processing program (like Microsoft Word or Pages) instead of a slideware program (like PowerPoint or Keynote). The company believes that writing ideas in complete sentences and paragraphs, rather than bullet points, forces a deeper clarity of thinking. Professor Edward Tufte, author of *The Cognitive Style of PowerPoint*, would likely agree. He believes that poor decision-making because of the overuse of bullet points via slideware negatively influenced decision-making and contributed to the Columbia shuttle disaster in 2003.

At Amazon, meetings can start with significant silence while everyone reads the document. The six-page memo provides a deep context of what's going to be discussed. When everyone is ready, discussion begins. Questions are asked and answered. A decision is made. In a blog post on LinkedIn, an Amazon executive says that this approach creates an incredible competitive advantage. By separating the written word from the spoken, "Amazon absolutely runs better, makes better decisions, and scales better because of this particular innovation."

The modern combination of slideware and projectors has led to the assumption that slides are free. And, technically, other than time to produce and electricity or paper to show, they cost nothing; each no longer costs seventy-five dollars to go from designer through film processing to audience. Type in your ideas, connect your device, and *voila!*

But slides are not free. The research is unequivocal. Every slide that's shown when someone is talking—every situation in which there's something for the audience to read, to think about, to decode or to decipher—comes with a cognitive cost. The price? Fewer of the presenter's ideas are heard, understood and retained by the audience.

In today's topsy-turvy world, slides no longer support the speaker; the speaker has become an add-on to the slides. The next time you attend a presentation online, ask yourself which is dominant: The speaker, or the slides? The audience does not or cannot hear what is said. Information dies a quick death at the presentation. It cannot be used or passed along to others. And the exercise of developing and delivering the presentation is a less-than-optimal use of everyone's time—for both presenter and audience.

I once wrote a blog item that suggested two changes to the next edition of slideware that would make the world a better place. The first is that there should be no font smaller than ninety-six-point on all-text slides, minimizing the words that can be crammed onto a single slide. (Graphs and charts would receive an exemption from this change, but not the second one.) I know what you're now thinking. You'll need at least a hundred slides to get your ideas across.

And that brings us to the second change. When you register any slideware program, you cannot use it until you connect it to an individual or organizational bank account. For each presentation, you receive a title slide and four additional slides at no charge. For every slide you use after that, fifty dollars is taken from your bank account and contributed to the charitable organization of your choice.

If we assume forty million presentations per day, each with a conservative average of thirty slides, we would have about fifty billion dollars per day donated to charitable causes worldwide. Of course, for those who don't want to donate per slide, the alternative is to employ only five slides for each presentation.

Either way, the world would be a better place.

S uppose you're hired to deliver the keynote presentation at a conference and you get stuck at an airport en-route. Could you email your slides and have someone flip through them on your behalf, while still collecting the fee? Not likely. I doubt that they'd even flip through your slides if you told them they could do so for free. The same applies with remote presentations. If your Internet slows to a crawl and you can stream neither audio nor video, but you've already sent your slides, would that cut it? No way.

Let's suppose you make it to the in-person presentation but the projector breaks down before the presentation begins, or the moderator at a remote event can't get your slides to share. Could you still deliver your presentation? Of course. Your slides are your notes and they're on your laptop (or tablet or smartphone or desktop). It's simply a matter of delivering the presentation without showing the slides.

The only reason for bringing everyone together is to listen to someone share something of value. Without slides, there can be a presentation. Without a presenter, there is no presentation. Successful presenters understand this. They know that capitalizing on how people listen is the key to their success—to having their ideas understood, absorbed, remembered and acted upon.

Listening involves both working memory and long-term memory. When we listen to someone, we take a small amount of information into working memory, which then interacts with long-term memory to find or create a place for that idea in our cognitive framework. The only ideas that have a hope of being remembered are those that make it to long-term memory. Everything else is forgotten.

When working memory is interacting with long-term memory, listening stops. During a conversation, if we're processing what someone has just said, or thinking about what we would like to say in exchange, we cannot listen to what the other person is now saying.

An example that demonstrates this is mobile phone use and driving. If we're making our way along the freeway with no traffic issues, of course we can listen to someone on the phone. But if something happens in front of us, we have a choice. We can continue listening, or we can think about what's in front of us. We cannot do both.

Some years ago, a North American insurance organization tested this concept. People were given an obstacle course to navigate. They went through the course the first time while focusing exclusively on driving and received a score. The second time through, they were told they had to continue a conversation on their phone while navigating the obstacle course, and received a second score. When the results were released, the scientist conducting the study started the news conference by saying: "We have proven that people cannot listen and think at the same time."

As humans, we can either listen to what someone is currently saying, or we can process what the person has just said. We cannot do both. If we're interrupted while moving what we've just heard to long-term memory, the information is lost, regardless of how important that information is to us.

If you've ever attended a fantastic presentation that provided incredible value, but the next day cannot remember a single detail about what you heard, you're familiar with working memory being overloaded and nothing being remembered. There were many great ideas to think about, but you were given no time to think about them. In the end, you retain little, if anything at all.

I once delivered a presentation to a conference for not-for-profit executives at a resort north of Toronto. My breakout presentation began after lunch, and I struck up a conversation as people filtered in. By the time a few people sat down, I asked: "How was the luncheon presentation?"

"Fantastic," they exclaimed. "There was so much she talked about that could benefit our agencies."

"Like what?" I asked.

What happened next was interesting, to say the least. It took them a few minutes to come up with anything. Because there was a non-stop stream of great information that was delivered so quickly, it spilled out and the audience had no chance to process anything. When I asked about the presentation a few minutes later, they could recall very little, even though they had just walked out of what they all believed was a fantastic talk of incredible value.

But someone remembered a small piece here and another there, so they could actually piece together an idea or two. But they were shocked at how little they recalled, and all agreed that if I hadn't motivated them to think about and discuss the presentation with my question, they would have remembered nothing when they returned to their agencies.

The relationship between working memory and long-term memory is the product of hundreds of thousands of years of human evolution. It will not change in our lifetimes. I recently watched a documentary in which a scientist surmised that humans have not evolved cognitively in any significant way in at least forty thousand years.

Working memory is small and fickle. It overloads quickly. And that's why nearly eighty-three per cent of us would rather do something else than attend another standard presentation, delivered one slide at a time. Standard presentations make listening a chore instead of a pleasure, and retention of information exceptionally difficult.

The best way to understand the relationship between working memory and long-term memory is to think of the sender of information (the presenter) as having a tank of water (the information for the presentation) that he or she would like to get across to a series of troughs, which represent the collective long-term memory of the audience. Logically, getting more water from tank to trough makes the presentation more memorable and ultimately more successful.

The audience has attended the presentation to learn or gain something. They want the information in the tank to be appropriate to their needs. To make best use of their time, they're looking for something of value—information that can help create a new trough or expand an existing one.

As the audience listens, they use working memory to transfer water from tank to trough. Working memory is the bucket that transfers ideas from tank to trough. And the bucket is truly small, more like a child's sandbox bucket than a milk bucket. It certainly isn't a five-gallon pail.

This means that the audience needs silence, and lots of it, to absorb what someone else says. Whoever is talking needs to pause frequently to allow those listening to move ideas from tank to bucket to trough, one small idea at a time. This, by the way, is the beginning of engagement. There simply is no engagement until working memory is actually working.

As we listen, we fill the bucket from the tank, walk it to our trough, deposit it, and return for another. Sounds simple, doesn't it?

But, in the vast majority of presentations, the tap is turned on and left on—delivering a non-stop stream of verbal information. In the vast majority of presentations, there is not a pause to be found anywhere. People fear "dead air." And they shouldn't. Dead air is the secret to influencing when the audience things and what they think about.

If the tap is running while the audience is on their way to or from the trough, what comes out of the tap (what the speaker says) is lost. If the audience is truly interested in the information, they'll keep trying to go back and forth, much like the not-for-profit executives I spoke with.

But if the information isn't that interesting, the audience quickly discovers that it will never go back and forth fast enough, so it figuratively finds a nearby stump on which to sit, sets its collective buckets on the ground, and does something else. This is where smartphones and laptops appear. They know they'll never absorb it all, so why try? I have been in rooms where every single person present is doing something else while the speaker drones on in the background.

Working memory is overloaded in two ways. It is overloaded when too much verbal information comes too quickly; there are no pauses with which the audience can process information as it flies by. Working memory is also overloaded any time spoken information is combined with written information—whether bullet points, sentences, paragraphs, charts or graphs. The vast majority of standard presentations overload working memory by doing both. There is a non-stop stream of verbal information accompanied by lots of slides to read.

To achieve success with any kind of presentation, you have to facilitate the process by which information goes from you to them, one bucket at a time. If you try to cram too much information into your presentation, you will have no choice but to open the tap and let it run. There won't be a pause anywhere. Rest assured that the vast majority of what you say will be lost.

People don't remember what you say. They remember what they thought about what you said—how they took your information and applied it to their trough, their individual frame of reference, their personal cognitive framework. When you understand how to tap into how they listen and remember, your ideas can be memorable years later.

I recently attended an annual conference of public relations professionals. During a social event, a conference participant looked at my name tag and said: "I was at your presentation 'The Fallacy of Staying on Message.' I still use the polarization model you shared. I can't tell you how helpful it's been."

As we talked, we realized that the presentation was delivered to the same conference ten years earlier. I remember planning that presentation. I knew about fifty to sixty public relations professionals would attend my breakout session. I brought enough information in my notes to fill exactly half the time frame, leaving lots of time for questions, which I encouraged and answered throughout the presentation. I easily answered fifty to sixty questions along the way and finished on time.

When I introduced the polarization model, I used a flip chart to draw it as I explained it. Essentially, I had the same conversation with conference attendees that I've had with thousands of clients one-on-one and in small media training workshops. In return, she was kind enough to still be applying my ideas ten years later.

What you say is the only place from which value can be derived from your presentations. If you want people to remember your ideas, you have to feed into how they listen. The secret to success is relatively simple: Provide interesting ideas for the audience to think about, turn off the tap, and give them time to think about each thought. Minimize the slides you use, if it's necessary to use any at all. Engage your audience in a structured conversation and more of what you say will be remembered.

AVOID BUCKET OVERLOAD

I once attended a presentation in which the presenter stated his objective was to get through fifty-one slides in fifty minutes. He turned on the tap and didn't touch it until the tank was bone dry. Within minutes, everyone was figuratively soaked and visibly doing something else. Though not a soul was listening, on he droned. He achieved his objective of getting through all his slides, but not a drop made it from tank to bucket, let alone trough.

During my presentation after lunch, as I was talking to the group about the value and advantages of conversational presentations, one of the participants said: "So what you're telling us is that the presentation before lunch was a complete waste of time."

I must admit my heart rate rose. The presenter's organization was paying my speaker's fee and travel expenses. However, I had two things in my favour. The first was that the presenter didn't stay for lunch or attend my session in the afternoon. The second was that I was speaking to a group of certified professionals who had to earn continuing education credits to maintain their licenses, so I asked: "Will you receive credits for attending that presentation?"

"Yes," he replied.

"From that perspective," I said, "this whole day has value." Fortunately, no one pressed the issue. But I don't think my heart rate went back to normal until later that night.

If what comes out of the speaker's mouth is where value can be found, visual aids should support the speaker, not the other way around. I have never, ever said that slides or other forms of visual aids shouldn't be used. Ever. When a visual is needed to aid understanding (such as a map, chart or graph, or even a critical quote, sentence, case study or paragraph), it should be used. However, when it is no longer needed, it should be removed from view and the conversation continued with the audience.

We have moved away from presentations as structured conversations, and we need to move back. It's time to let go of the basic assumption that showing slides during a speech or presentation is somehow more effective than simply talking to people. It isn't. Research has consistently shown that standard presentations are ultimately less effective than the alternative of conversing with the audience. In other words, the way in which most presentations are delivered, one slide at a time, is the least effective way to communicate if you want your ideas to be heard, understood, retained, applied and acted upon.

In 2007, a research team from the University of New South Wales, led by John Sweller, PhD, released a study that concluded that when humans attempt to read and listen at the same time, working memory is overloaded and they retain less than if they either read or listen separately. And this has consistently been verified by research at a variety of universities around the world.

Researchers at Purdue University concluded it's possible to "hear" more of what a professor says by not attending class, than attending a class in which slides are shown. This study was conducted among students enrolled in a course entitled "Human Factors in Engineering," which was delivered to students from four majors: engineering, humanities, management and technology. The course was attended by undergraduate and graduate students and was taught three times a week for sixteen weeks.

There were two separate streams of classes for the course, which was based on the textbook *Human Factors in Simple and Complex Systems*. For two identical lectures, two different delivery styles were used with exactly the same information presented. One lecture showed slides. One did not. The lecture that didn't show slides employed a chalkboard or whiteboard where necessary to highlight visual concepts— commonly known as "chalk and talk" in academic circles. The other used slides.

Researchers then used a twenty-question, multiple-choice quiz to test students' ability to recall information from the lecture in four categories: oral information, graphic information, alphanumeric information, and information presented orally with visual support.

The researchers' first hypothesis was that using slides would have a negative effect on what was said. They believed that students who saw the slides would have lower scores on oral comprehension. This was confirmed. Students who didn't see slides scored twenty-nine per cent higher in recalling oral information, and achieved higher overall scores with the recall of all information. "The presence of PowerPoint negatively affected the recall of auditory information," the researchers said, adding that "graphic scores reveal there was no notable gain when using PowerPoint to display graphic information."

Students scored just as high on graphic recall when professors used the chalkboard when needed, rather than showing slides. The slides added zero value, and had a decidedly negative effect on the ability to listen to what was said.

In addition to testing students who attended the lectures with and without slides, the researchers discovered they were testing a third group: those who didn't attend either class but showed up to write the quiz. These students did their work outside of class. Interestingly, those who read the textbook, did their work outside the classroom and showed up to write the quiz scored higher on oral comprehension than those who attended the PowerPoint lecture. They "heard" more by not attending class, than attending the class in which slides were shown.

R esearchers from Universitat Autònoma de Barcelona in Spain concluded that slides impede communication, leading to lower retention by the audience. However, this study also addressed the belief that, when using slides, the slides themselves are not the problem. If people knew how to use slideware properly, this argument goes, there wouldn't be a problem. "PowerPoint doesn't bore people," these folks often say. "Using PowerPoint poorly is what bores people."

Not true. The Barcelona study demonstrated that eliminating slides improves both average and good presenters, which is something I've known for decades (and is something we'll discuss in greater detail later). In this particular study, while one professor's students scored higher overall than the other—i.e. one lecturer was a better presenter than the other—the students of both professors who saw slides scored significantly lower than those who didn't.

The Barcelona study was conducted with a base of two-hundred-and-five students registered in a course entitled "The Psychology of Education." This was a compulsory course for those working toward a bachelor's degree in psychology.

Students were divided into four streams led by two professors. On different days, each professor taught one stream of students in the morning and one in the afternoon. For this study, each professor used slides for one class and a blackboard for the other.

The professors worked together to develop a nineteen-slide, forty-minute presentation for the class in which slides would be shown—fairly "standard" slides that all of us have seen more times than we can count. They also prepared a ten-question multiple-choice quiz to evaluate the knowledge students acquired from the lecture. The test was administered immediately after each of the four lectures and based solely on information taught during class.

Students who didn't see slides scored twenty-two per cent higher on the quiz than those who did. By simply shutting off the projector, communication effectiveness can be enhanced by twenty-two per cent (and that's without implementing a single additional idea from this book).

Researchers at Ludwig-Maximilians-Universität München, led by Professor Christoph Wecker, confirmed the results of the studies at Purdue and Barcelona. Dr. Wecker's team tested two types of slides—what they called "regular" and "concise" slides—versus just talking to the audience. The researchers concluded that the retention of oral information was significantly lower during lectures that used regular slides compared to lectures without slides.

Professor Wecker calls this a speech suppression effect. If you buy into the argument that presentation value comes from what the presenter says, suppressing spoken information is counterproductive. Significantly less makes it from tank to trough, which negatively impacts communication effectiveness.

However, if the audience loses a large portion of what's said while slides are shown, is there an offsetting gain to using slides? If slides take away from communication effectiveness in one area, do they add value somewhere else?

Dr. Wecker's team determined the answer to both questions is an unequivocal no. "It is remarkable, however, that this 'suppressive' effect of regular slides," they said, "could not be demonstrated to be the downside of a trade-off in favour of the retention of information on slides."

When presentations use what the researchers call regular slides (of precisely the same density—the same number of letters and words—as the slide to the right), audiences lose huge portions of what is said. And the communication effectiveness lost by showing slides is not regained anywhere else, leading to a net negative impact of

University of Munich Study
Sample "Regular" Slide

using slides. I changed the words on this slide into gibberish, but this was the exact density of a slide in the study. With about thirty-five words each, Professor Wecker's regular slides are almost identical to the six-by-six guideline (six lines of text with six words per line) that many presenters have adopted for slides. Dr. Wecker demonstrated that the six-by-six approach significantly decreases a presenter's ability to move information from tank to trough.

The researchers also tested what they called concise slides. This lecture, with slides identical in density to the slide shown at the right, used six slides (four fewer than the presentation with standard slides): a title slide, a structural slide, and four additional slides. None of the concise slides contained more than seven lines (excluding the heading) or five bullet points. The example on this page has twelve words.

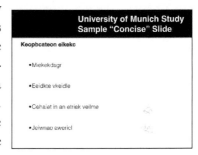

The researchers also used "black" slides between the regular slides, attempting to create somewhat of a hybrid between standard and conversational presentations. However, while the hybrid improved communication outcomes when compared to standard slides, nothing worked better than removing slides from view. Bullet points, even those as skimpy as what's shown on the slide above, overload working memory.

What does this mean for you? You have a choice. You can continue to show bullet points, quotes, sentences and paragraphs to the audience. If you do, the message is one hundred percent clear: your communication effectiveness will be negatively impacted. People will forget what you've said as soon as you're done.

Alternatively, you can choose to set yourself and your ideas apart by focusing on having a conversation with the audience. As we'll discuss in the next chapter, use notes to keep yourself on track and on time. But don't show your notes to the audience. When you need a visual to aid understanding, use it. But when it's no longer needed, remove it from view and carry on the conversation.

F or those who like using a lot of charts and graphs during presentations, the news is grim. When shown while someone is speaking, charts and graphs overload working memory. Always. Anyone who has sat through a presentation of charts and graphs knows how mentally and emotionally laborious this can become, and how little is ultimately retained.

Charts and graphs are data that can best be shared in a written document, either before or after the presentation. Effective presenters tell the story that connects the dots. What does the data mean? Why is it important? How will it affect the audience? How can better decisions be made as a result of the data that's available?

Data is the spice. The story of how everything fits together is the main meal. However, like any spice, too much data can ruin the meal.

If they must be used during a presentation (and they should always be used sparingly), charts and graphs are more effective when the audience's cognitive framework is first pointed in the right direction. While the significance of the visual is explained, it should not be visible, either on-screen or on paper. When the visual is shown, in silence, the audience can reconcile what they've just heard with what they now see. This improves understanding and retention.

Perhaps an example will explain this concept. Suppose I'm an architect, and your firm has hired me to design a new building. The facility will house your corporate offices and include a large warehouse as a major shipping hub. A number of your executives provided insight into their requirements as part of the design process.

The vice-president of human resources told me that one of his primary wishes was to have a bright and cheerful reception area. "It's the first thing our customers, suppliers, employees and visitors see," he said. "I want the reception area to make a positive first impression on everyone who comes here."

The vice-president of product and service development said that her biggest concern is creating an environment conducive to teamwork. Any work space for her group must be extremely flexible. There may be situations in which teams need to be assembled on a moment's notice. Other times, groups may work together for weeks.

The vice-president of distribution had still different concerns. "The doors on our loading dock are too narrow," she said during one of our meetings. "It's difficult to get product in and out. A bright reception area is nice and flexible work space is important, but I need wider doors on our loading dock. As we grow, moving product in and out will become critical."

I make note of these thoughts and more, then return to my office to design a new building. Once my design is complete, I have some choices on how to present my solution to the senior management team. One of these is: What should I use as a visual aid during my presentation to the client? After exploring my options, I decide to construct a scale model of the building.

At the start of my presentation, I explain that I have positioned the building on the footprint of the land facing southwest. I built the reception area out from the main building and enclosed it in glass—UV protective glass, so the receptionist and visitors will not be required to wear sunscreen. However, if there is even a hint of sunshine, the reception area will be warm and friendly.

To address the teamwork issue, I tell the audience I partnered with an office design firm that specializes in creating flexible workspaces. The upper floor of the office building will be co-designed by this company. Staff will be able to easily move furniture on a moment's notice. Most of the walls can be arranged to create private, semi-private or open concept workspaces quickly and easily.

Finally, the way I positioned the building on the footprint of the land enabled me to make excellent use of available space. Not only did I provide extra-wide doors on the loading dock, I was able to expand the size of the loading dock and include five additional doors.

During my presentation, while I'm talking about how the building I've designed meets their needs, should the model be in plain view or out of view? Should the audience be able to see it while I'm talking about it? Or should the focus be entirely on me and what I'm saying?

I believe the model should be out of view or covered. If it's visible, the management team will look at it. They will examine it. Working memory and long-term memory will be engaged, leaving little room, if any, to process what I'm saying.

While I'm describing their new building, I would encourage questions but would keep my answers brief, which we'll talk about later. When I complete my description and answer all questions, I would uncover the model and step back.

There is no value to interrupting their thoughts, so I will pause and say nothing until they are done examining the model, regardless of how long that pause feels to me or how uncomfortable I become. At the very least, I should not say another word until at least half of them look up from the model, or someone asks a question.

This process should be applied any time a chart or graph is shown to any audience. And no presentation should ever contain more than four or five charts or graphs. Maximum.

With the screen blank, tell the audience what they're going to see. Help them understand the significance of the visual, the interrelationships of it, then reveal it. When they're examining it, stop talking. Wait. Anything you say will be wasted, and will interfere with their ability to digest what they're seeing. When they're ready, answer any questions, blank the screen, and move on.

If you tell someone you're using visual aids for your presentation, chances are they'll automatically think of PowerPoint or some other slideware program. But this is too limiting. We have a range of tools at our disposal, which can be used to influence the ways in which information is transferred from tank to trough. The appropriate tool needs to be applied to each specific challenge if the goal is to communicate effectively. Slides are one tool, but not the only one.

In a YouTube video, for example, a consultant uses a lemon to explain successful negotiation. "Seems pretty simple," he says. "I have two parties, party A and party B. Both want the lemon." He cuts the lemon. "I give the two parties to this dispute fifty per cent of the available resources. You'd think they would be happy."

But they are not happy. They cannot achieve fifty per cent of their goals. In fact, when he probes, he discovers neither can achieve anything.

However, by listening to their concerns, he realizes that one party wants to make lemonade and needs the juice from the lemon. "That's pretty easy," he explains, reaching for another prop. "I've got a juicer and that party can be satisfied."

He discovers the other party wants to make a cake with lemon frosting and only needs the rind. He picks up another tool. "By peeling the lemon, (one) party can be one hundred per cent satisfied," he concludes. "And by juicing the lemon, (the other) party can be one hundred per cent satisfied—when there was no satisfaction before."

Is this consultant using a visual aid? Of course he is; he is using a number of them—lemon, knife, juicer and peeler—to support his talk. But, in a true test of communication effectiveness, he could deliver exactly the same presentation whether he is talking to one person or ten thousand. In fact, he could deliver a very similar presentation over the telephone or during a conference call and still communicate effectively.

If he was delivering the presentation to a room of a thousand people, the audio-visual company could use a video camera to capture him using his props, and project that image onto a large screen behind him. That way, everyone in the room would have an unobstructed view of his demonstration. This is part of the staging process that helped Steve Jobs become an admired presenter. His ultimate secret? He never let a slide—any slide—get between him and his audience.

Marshall McLuhan introduced us to "the medium is the message." The idea is that the form of communication someone uses shapes how the message is communicated and perceived. Depending on whether a perception needs to be created, reinforced or changed, as well as the audience's characteristics and need for information, there are a variety of tools to help us inform or influence others—tools that can enhance and improve how water is transferred from tank to trough. They range from a scale model, a knife, a juicer and a lemon to flip charts, whiteboards and a blank piece of paper between salesperson and client, to charts, graphs, printed income statements, balance sheets and spreadsheets with dozens of cells that can be handed to the audience when needed. Slides are somewhere on that list, but they are not the only tool that can or should be used.

Imagine that the mechanic where you get your vehicle serviced has only one tool to complete the job. Can he or she successfully fix your vehicle using only a screwdriver or crescent wrench? Possibly, but probably not. By the same token, if you limit your toolbox to slides, be prepared to limit your success.

For every visual aid you use, ask yourself two questions: Is it absolutely necessary? Will it interfere with the conversation?

To avoid overloading working memory, the answers to these questions must be "yes" and "no," respectively. Yes, the visual is absolutely necessary to help the audience understand. (By the way, bullet points almost never are.) And no, it doesn't interfere with the conversation. (Bullet points always do.) Only then should it be included. If the visual isn't absolutely necessary, or if it will interfere with the conversation in any way, blank the screen and simply talk to your audueince. It is your best chance at having your ideas remembered, applied and acted upon.

SHAPE THE TANK

I wrote my first speech for a senior executive less than a year after starting my communications career in June1982. It was a five-minute speech for an assistant deputy minister in the government department at which I worked. He was attending a retirement event and had been asked to say a few words. Even though the stakes were not high, I worked five hours to craft that five minutes.

I researched the Latin signature of the university at which the event was being held (and from which the honoured guest was retiring as the dean of education). I translated the university's Latin inscription of *quaecumque vera* into "whatsoever things are true" so it could be included in the speech. I also spoke with a faculty member in the university's Latin studies department, who taught me how to pronounce the inscription correctly. I, in turn, taught my speaker.

Apparently, it went well. I received a lovely thank you note from the speaker, which I still have, and I wrote a number of speeches for him before moving to another job a year or so later. A year after that, on September 17, 1985, thirty-five years to the day before the publication of this book, I left government and set out on my own as a freelance communications consultant.

For the first eight years of my freelance life, I wrote hundreds of speeches for politicians, bureaucrats and executives in corporate, government and not-for-profit sectors. I discovered that freelance speechwriting is a fascinating business model. The client is willing to spend a specific amount of money to generate a speech for a specific event. If things don't go smoothly, the client is generally not willing to spend more money. In almost every case, the speechwriter eats the difference.

As a speechwriter, if I spent more hours crafting the speech, I earned less per hour on average. If I spent fewer hours writing the speech, my average hourly income rose proportionately. From a business perspective, therefore, the goal was to deliver an excellent product in the fewest possible hours.

The client group (and it was often a group) would provide background for the speech. This was where I first learned that there is always more information than time. Sometimes I would receive a virtual mountain of information that might include annual reports, newsletters, news releases, feature articles, previous speeches, and other documents. We would have a discussion about the direction the speech should take. I would then go away to write it.

I would toil and trouble. I would write and re-write. When I was done toiling, troubling, writing and re-writing, I would send a draft to the client. Early in my career, and more often than not, the client would start our review by saying "we think the draft is really well written, thank you for that, but it's not what we want to say." And I would try again. It was a frustrating process.

My frustration peaked during an assignment in which I wrote a speech for the Canadian CEO of a Japanese automobile manufacturer. Every member of the content team said they knew what the CEO wanted to say. After the meeting, I gathered up the information they provided and, over a week or so, wrote a speech that reflected what was discussed.

The approval process went smoothly. I had learned many lessons during the previous five or six years, or so I thought. Everyone agreed the speech was well written. After a few changes, the group approved the draft and sent it to the CEO.

The next day, my business partner called me out of a meeting I was attending at another client's office. "The CEO didn't like the speech," my partner told me over the phone. "He'd like you to call him at four o'clock this afternoon to provide you with some insight."

I called the CEO that afternoon. In less than an hour, he provided fantastic input into what he would like to say. It was the start of a wonderful working relationship that lasted until he retired and returned to Japan.

At the end of our conversation, he said: "I don't mean to cause you a problem, but I have a flight to Japan tomorrow. Could you please send a draft of the speech to my office by nine am?"

It was Halloween night. After dinner, my spouse and I took our kids out trick-or-treating, then I went to the office to re-write the speech.

At about four o'clock in the morning, I vowed that one of two things would happen. Either I would find a better way to write speeches, or I would find another way to make a living. From this experience, the basic presentation framework was born.

The basic presentation framework forces a discipline in which the entire speech or presentation is clearly stated in six to eight sentences. The framework outlines the beginning, middle and end of the journey the audience will take, and is the foundation on which subsequent content is constructed. It provides a focal point to shape content to the needs of each specific audience. And it embeds a call to action that supports the presenter's business and communication objectives.

I used the framework to significantly improve the finished speeches I delivered. It decreased the time necessary to develop effective content—cutting the hours needed by at least half, if not more. I have taught this process to clients during presentation skills workshops for more than twenty-five years. I have clients who have used it for decades.

The premise of the framework is simple: If you can't communicate your ideas clearly in six simple sentences, a sixty-minute time frame will never ride to your rescue. If your ideas aren't clear in the shorter format, they'll never be clear in the longer one.

Within my content development process, once the framework was complete and approved, the next step was to transfer the information and create a notes outline. Once that was approved, I would expand the outline to fit the time frame needed. Lastly, visual aids would be developed.

My meetings to develop speeches (and all presentations since) changed once I began using the framework. I started the content development process by drawing a horizontal rectangular box at the top of a flip chart or whiteboard, or a piece of paper if working with someone one-on-one. The goal is to fill that box with the main theme of the speech or presentation in one simple sentence. This sentence always contains the word "why" or "how"—as in "I'd like to talk to you about how ..." or "I'm here to share why ..."

Using "how" or "why" does two things. It helps the audience put information into context, shaping the tank to make ideas easier to follow, understand and remember. For example, starting a presentation by saying "I'd like to talk to you about the basic presentation framework" means nothing to anyone. Starting with "I'd like to talk to you about *how* the basic presentation framework can save you time in developing any presentation" or "I'd like to talk to about *why* the basic presentation framework will help you significantly increase your sales success" helps the audience understand the ways in which information should be considered as it's moved from tank to trough.

The second reason for using "how" or "why" is that it reminds speakers that they are there to put information into perspective, not download data. Many successful presentations use some data, but have a clear statement of purpose that puts the sprinkling of data into a meaningful frame of reference.

Once everyone agrees on the first sentence (and only after everyone agrees), I draw five narrow horizontal boxes under the first, explaining as I do that our goal is to put one sentence into each box. The top two boxes form the introduction, the next three are the main body, and the last is the conclusion. Once the framework is complete, someone (such as your boss, your client or your spouse) should be able to understand the ground your presentation will cover by simply reading the framework. There is no depth, but the story will have a clear beginning, middle and end.

Some might call this a version of the "tell them what you're going to tell them, tell them, and tell them what you've told them" formula. Unfortunately, the application of this well-known adage often translates into "tell them you're going to be boring, be boring, and if anyone's still awake, tell them you were boring at the end."

The first defence against boredom is to begin at the end and bring that end to the beginning. Start with a clear call to action. What do you want the audience to do or not do as a result of what they're about to hear?

In an informative presentation, the call to action is to apply the information in the presentation in a meaningful way, such as "my goal is to help you understand what we're doing so our teams don't overlap as they approach customers." The call to action in persuasive presentation should encourage direct action, as in "at the end of this discussion, we will be seeking your approval for the budget this project requires."

The second horizontal box contains the call to action in one clear, simple sentence. Occasionally, you may need two, but strive to keep it to one.

The next challenge is to put one sentence into each of the next three boxes to frame the presentation's main content. Each sentence should represent one section of the main body. It should be simple and declarative. And it must directly support the two boxes at the top of the framework. If a sentence in the main body doesn't support the statement of purpose or the call to action, there are two choices. Adjust the statement of purpose or the call to action, or adjust the sentence in the main body. By stripping ideas down to a framework, you can quickly determine whether the pieces actually fit together.

The last box forms the conclusion, which succinctly recaps the three main ideas in the body of the presentation and restates the call to action. Using a loose syllogism is often a very effective way of concluding. "Because of this, because of that and because of this third thing, you should be motivated to apply the information I've provided and/or take the action I'm seeking."

Two examples of the framework follow. The first describes what should be in each box. The second applies the framework to a presentation about how the framework can be used to generate sales results.

> *This is the main theme of the presentation in one sentence that should contain "how" or "why."*

> *The call to action is stated clearly and concisely in one to two simple sentences.*

> *This is the first main section of the presentation, which should be stated in one clear sentence.*

> *This is the second main section of the presentation.*

> *This is the third main section of the presentation.*

> *This is the conclusion, in which the main points are recapped and the call to action restated. Using a loose syllogism is often an effective way to do this.*

I'd like to talk about how the basic presentation framework can help you generate better results from the sales presentations you deliver.

By the end of our discussion, my goal is to convince you to use the framework when developing any sales presentation. Whether you're talking to a single prospect or a group, it's an important tool to help hit your targets.

The framework helps you focus and clarify your ideas.

The framework makes it easier for the audience to understand and retain your ideas.

Better understanding and retention equal better sales results.

Because the framework helps you focus and clarify your ideas ... because it makes it easier for the audience to understand and retain your ideas ... and because better understanding and retention equal better sales results ... I strongly encourage you to apply the framework to every sales presentation you deliver in the future. It will help you hit your targets.

During speechwriting assignments, once the framework was approved by the content team and the speaker, the next step was to create an outline. I would do this by skimming the written information I had been provided, or reviewing notes I'd taken during the meeting. The outline for speeches would be written in full sentences, and be about one-and-a-half pages in length—four hundred words or less using full sentences. (Sentences were appropriate for speechwriting; the speaker would read his or her speech from full sentences.) The outline would be sent to the content team and speaker for approval.

The example that follows uses notes, which are appropriate for presentations that are not going to be read word-for-word. My clients have often referred to them as stripped-down sentences. These notes can be used as a five-minute version of the presentation and, like the outline written in full sentences, can also be sent to others for approval. I recommend that my clients deliver their presentations from notes very similar to these, never from full and complete sentences.

In fact, when you expand your content beyond the framework, leave sentences behind. Using notes speeds up the thought process and supports a conversational delivery. Sentences get bogged down in wordsmithing along the way and almost always come across as slow, stilted and robotic when delivered.

If you deliver the notes below the way we'll discuss in the next chapter, this will be almost exactly four minutes of information, regardless of who is delivering it. We'll refer to these notes again when we talk about the basic pattern that occurs in relaxed conversation, so you might want to bookmark this page.

- Like talk how basic presentation framework generate better results every sales presentation deliver future.
- By end discussion, my goal convince you start with framework when developing sales presentations.
  - Whether 1-on1 / groups—important tool help hit targets.
- Talk three points to get us there:
  - Framework helps you focus / clarify ideas.
  - Framework makes easier for audience understand / retain ideas.
  - Better understanding / retention = better sales results.

- Framework helps you focus / clarify ideas.
  - One size not fit all in presentations / each audience different.
  - Enable quickly customize info each audience needs.
  - Information shaped fit audience / story has clear beginning, middle, end.

- Framework makes easier for audience understand / retain ideas.
  - Ideas focused on their needs — directly relevant their need understand.
  - By having clear statement purpose / call to action, audience put ideas into context as come across.
  - Notes help you convey ideas one at a time / making easier go from you to their long-term memory.

- Better understanding / retention = better sales results.
  - All things equal, better understand and retain your ideas / more confident purchasing from you.
  - By better remember your ideas / prospect & clients favourably compare your ideas to competitors.
  - By planting ideas firmly their minds, make easier them to pick you.

- In conclusion, because framework helps you focus / clarify your ideas ...
  - Because make easier for them understand / retain your ideas ...
  - Because better understanding / retention = better sales results ...
- I encourage you start with framework when developing presentations ...
  - As important tool help hit sales targets.

Taking time to create an outline is an important intermediate step to ensure that the presentation stays focused on its original intent. It helps determine whether the presentation supports the business and communication objectives you want to achieve. And you can verify that it's something you (or someone else if you're not the speaker) actually wants to say. It's a great step in any approval process.

Once the outline was approved by the content team and the speaker, I would return to the information I received from the client to find the pieces appropriate to expand the content. As you expand, remember that there is always more information than time. If you have ten minutes, you can undoubtedly find enough information for twenty. If you have an hour, chances are can find enough for two. But the amount of information that can be included in any presentation is dictated by the time available. Period. And, as you shape the tank, leave at least one-third to one-half of the available time for questions from the audience.

Ideally, questions should be encouraged and answered throughout presentations, which is something we'll discuss in greater detail later. At a minimum, questions should be encouraged at the end of each section of the presentation wherever and whenever remotely possible. This may be difficult with an audience of five thousand, but answering questions at the end of each section with audiences of less than a hundred or during a webinar should be mandatory. With audiences of fewer than fifty, questions should be answered throughout the presentation.

Without some form of back-and-forth between presenter and audience, what on earth is the purpose of getting together? You might as well record a video of yourself delivering the presentation, load it and hit play. Then, if you wish, you can answer questions when the video concludes.

If you have an hour, bring thirty minutes of information. If you say everything you need to say, answer one or two dozen questions from the audience, motivate them to apply or take action on your ideas, and finish a few minutes early, who will ever complain?

As you expand the notes outline, stay true to the framework and cover the same ground as the five-minute version, but at a deeper level. Be judicious and selective with the data you bring. Use examples, anecdotes, stories, comparisons and case studies to breathe life into data and shape your ideas for the audience.

You may include some form of creative opening at the beginning, such as a story or a quick poll of the audience. But any form of creative opening (or any jokes, for that matter) must be directly related to the main theme and the call to action. If not, you run the risk of having them remember the joke or creative opening, but little else.

In the absence of a creative opening, there is absolutely nothing wrong with starting with the brief, simple introduction shown in the notes. It gets to the point. It provides a clear link to how the information will benefit the audience. It gives people a reason to sit up and listen.

When your content is complete, ask yourself one final question: Where is a visual absolutely necessary to support my ideas and motivate the audience? Develop visuals last, not first, if you wish to enhance your ability to have audiences understand and retain your ideas.

During the last few years I wrote speeches, the framework made it much easier to focus the content, the content team and the speaker on what's appropriate for that audience at that moment in time. The framework came with me as my career evolved to training and consulting, and it has been a core component of my presentation skills training program for more than twenty-five years.

When slides became readily available thirty years ago, the business model for speechwriting changed. My business partner and I worked with a designer who cracked the "rasterization" process with a small investment in hardware and software. She was able to inexpensively transfer the colour slide shown on her computer screen to an imprint on 35-mm film. Our raw cost per slide was three dollars, and customers happily purchased them for thirty-five dollars each.

When the speech was approved, I would open my early version of Power-Point or Cricket Presents on my black-and-white Macintosh Plus and type in bullet points to accompany the speech. Once the client approved the content for the slides, I would download the file to a three-and-a-half-inch floppy disk and courier it to the designer or drop it off at her home studio. The entire process generally took less than two hours.

She would load the content into a template previously approved by the client, rasterize the slides, and courier the film to a processing facility the next day. In our process, a five-slide build was actually five slides, each of which cost thirty-five dollars. Each speech, with builds, was easily accompanied by thirty to fifty slides.

At that time, the going rate for speeches was fifteen hundred to twenty-five hundred dollars. Even with the framework and my process, this represented between twelve and twenty hours of input. For the slides, the designer and I split the gross profit of thirty-two dollars per slide, which represented no more than three or four hours of input for both of us.

My business partner and I had visions of dollars signs dancing in our heads. We were developing relationships with suppliers to provide design and development services to clients seeking visual support for speeches and presentations we had written and were written by others. This was in the early 1990s, just as PowerPoint began taking the world by storm.

But over the span of a couple of years, I noticed that speeches accompanied by slides were more difficult to follow than those without slides. This occurred during rehearsals and the events themselves. After I saw a demonstration that separated the written word from the spoken using charts and graphs, similar to the architectural example from the previous chapter, I was hooked. I haven't looked at presentations the same way since.

For more than a quarter century, people have frequently asked why I don't like slides. It's not that I don't like slides. It's that I know communication can be so much more interesting and effective when slides are developed last, not first, in the content development process.

Successful presentations are based on a clear definition of precisely what the audience needs to understand for this presentation to be memorable. They shape the tank to bring value to that specific audience at that moment in time. They strive to make the audience's experience worth the effort.

When slideware drives content, the result is inevitable: There are too many slides with too much information on each. And, in this, the research is absolutely clear. Significantly less makes it to the collective long-term memory of those in attendance.

If you take one idea away from this book, I hope it's this: Using a slideware program to develop content doesn't work. It never has. It never will.

It is the root cause of 'Death by PowerPoint.' It should be avoided at all costs if your goal is to be meaningful and, ultimately, memorable.

FILL THE BUCKET

We have now arrived at another fundamentally incorrect assumption about presentations that needs to be debunked before we can go much further. There is absolutely no way that ninety-three per cent of communication is non-verbal. If it were, we'd be able to watch a foreign-language film, listen to how the words sound as the actors say them, watch how they look when they say the words, and understand ninety-three percent of what transpires. We'll see action and recognize emotion, but if we don't understand the words, we comprehend little.

The ninety-three per cent assumption comes from research conducted at Stanford University by Albert Mehrabian, published in the book *Silent Messages*. Professor Mehrabian first coined the 55-38-7 per cent statistic, which has been widely misinterpreted as fifty-five per cent of the message coming from how the person looks when saying the words, thirty-eight per cent of the message coming from how the words sound when spoken, and seven per cent comes from the words themselves.

I wrote a blog item nearly twenty years ago entitled "The Mehrabian Myth ... So much for 55, 38 & 7" that has taken on a life of its own. If you're interested in learning more, Google "Mehrabian myth." Be sure to watch the entertaining YouTube video that explains the myth perfectly. Your search will undoubtedly uncover that even Mehrabian refutes this misinterpretation of his research.

Professor Mehrabian's focus was credibility, not communication. He concluded that words, voice and gestures must work together in harmony. If they are inconsistent, listeners rely on more than what's said to determine whether the message should be believed. And that's common sense. When it looks as if someone is insincere, we watch and listen more carefully to determine whether we should trust them and their ideas.

A nd that brings us to another incorrect assumption about presentations. Body language is not a language. You can demonstrate discomfort, but until you communicate an idea, I will not know the cause. For example, your body language may indicate that you are experiencing discomfort. But until you use written language, spoken language or sign language to send me a message, I may not understand that you need the washroom. Likewise, I cannot direct you to the washroom by simply showing emotion, no matter how sad I am about your current plight. I have to use written language, spoken language or sign language to point you in the right direction.

For speeches and presentations, a more appropriate term than body language is "the use of gestures." And the best place to look for insight into how gestures help us communicate is the work of psycholinguists. These social scientists study the interrelationships between thought, gestures and our ability to communicate.

Psycholinguists have determined that people from every culture on the planet use gestures when they express themselves. It's something we all have in common. Psycholinguists have concluded that regardless of who we are or where we're from, we communicate best when we create unconscious, spontaneous gestures. In other words, the best "body language" advice you can ever receive is two words: be yourself. How you gesture and communicate should be very similar, whether you're talking on the telephone, sitting across the desk from someone or delivering a keynote address to thousands. The level of formality will vary, but the gestures themselves must be natural—spontaneous and unconscious.

In her book *Hearing Gesture: How our hands help us think*, psycholinguist Dr. Susan Goldin-Meadow writes that gestures are so much a part of the human condition that someone does not have to be sighted to use gestures. In her book, she describes an experiment in which teens blind from birth participated in a series of conversational tasks. All of them used gestures. "The blind group gestured at the same rate as the sighted group," she writes, "and conveyed the same information using the same range of gesture forms."

According to Dr. Goldin-Meadow: "Several types of evidence lend support to the view that gesture and speech form a single, unified system. The gestures speakers produce along with their talk are symbolic acts that convey meaning," which is why there is added value to face-to-face meetings or video calls versus telephone conversations. Audiences get more from the message if they're looking at the person talking while she or he is speaking.

Dr. Goldin-Meadow also believes that the use of gestures enhances thought processes. "When the act of speaking becomes difficult, speakers seem to respond by increasing their gestures," she writes. Attempting to reduce or eliminate gestures during presentations makes it more difficult to think of what you're trying to say during a time when you truly need your wits about you.

Professor Goldin-Meadow believes that to "ignore gesture is to ignore part of the conversation." She concludes that the very act of gesturing facilitates communication and promotes spatial thinking, and that stifling gestures inhibits someone's ability to think.

"At the very least," she says, "we ought to stop telling people not to move their hands when they talk."

If you gesture when you talk to someone on the telephone (and virtually all of us do), ask yourself: "Who are those gestures for?" Bring those gestures to your presentations and let them happen naturally. They're an integral component of who you are as a human being and how you communicate most effectively.

Natural gestures ensure consistency between the words spoken, how you sound when they're spoken and how you look when they're spoken. Natural gestures enhance your ability to think on your feet. They improve your ability to communicate effectively, which enables your audience to focus on filling their bucket instead of figuring out what you're doing with your hands. Natural gestures are such a part of your personality that the audience may not even notice them, even when you're doing something generally considered to be incorrect.

A number of years ago, I provided a full day of media training for an organization that was potentially facing a strike. The training was for management-level employees who might be called upon to deal with journalists at strike sites. At the start of the day, the company's director of human resources spent about forty-five minutes talking to the group about what was expected of them. She was an excellent communicator. She conducted a structured conversation with the group and answered all of their questions.

Later, when we discussed the use of gestures during TV interviews, I crossed my arms and asked if it was appropriate. No, they said, someone looks closed when they cross their arms.

I turned to the HR director and asked if she would ever stand in front of a group, present information and answer questions with her arms crossed. She said she would not. I asked the group of twenty-plus people if she would ever do that, and they all said that she was far too professional to ever cross her arms while standing in front of a group.

However, I was sitting at the back of the room with my video camera on a tripod while she did, so I quietly recorded her. When I played back the recording, everyone was surprised that they didn't notice she had committed a presentation *faux pas*.

But because the HR director was communicating naturally, they didn't mentally record her gestures. She was being herself. Her gestures were consistent with who she is as a person. If she was standing outside the room having a conversation with someone, she would be exactly the same person we saw talking to the group. And her arms may very well be crossed.

During her presentation, the HR director fulfilled two basic goals that all presenters should strive to achieve. First, she conveyed her message. Embedded within her message was a call to action. She was absolutely clear about what she wanted them to do. In any form of business-type presentation—lecture, speech, webinar, training program, business pitch, internal presentation, conference presentation or other—if you don't want the audience to apply or take action on the information, why bother?

Second, she conveyed her personality—who she is as an individual and a professional. Like all of us, if the medium is the message, her personality is the window through which the message must travel to be received, understood and acted upon by the audience.

Each of us conveys our message and personality every day of our lives during relaxed conversation. Relaxed conversation is our best possible presentation style. It is the secret to filling the bucket, one bucket at a time. It is the key to having our ideas understood, remembered, applied, acted upon, and passed along to others.

Perhaps an example will put this into perspective. Let's suppose you have a 1:00 p.m. meeting at the office of a colleague, client or boss. When you arrive, you both realize you haven't eaten. You decide to make it a working lunch. You're presenting an idea to the other person, which is the reason for getting together. Your goal is to obtain buy-in or approval. You finish lunch, then devote fifteen or twenty minutes to the business at hand.

Would you be able to talk intelligently to the other person about your idea? Of course. Would you have prepared in advance? Probably. Would you get buy-in? Maybe. Maybe not. A variety of factors could determine that. But let's suppose you do.

How many slides did you need to explain your ideas? None. I doubt that you would even think to use them. You might draw a picture on a napkin or piece of paper to aid understanding, if necessary, but you would simply carry on the conversation.

You did most of the talking because you were presenting the idea. But you didn't talk non-stop. After each idea, you looked for a nod or listened for an "uh-huh." If your lunch partner was visibly processing what you just said, you stopped talking and waited. You know that he or she cannot think and listen at the same time.

If your lunch partner had a question, you answered it. You didn't suggest that it be saved until after all of your information had been presented. Over lunch, you created a two-way process during which the speed at which information went from you to your partner was driven by her or his need to understand, not your need to get through it all. Your presentation was two-way and receiver-driven.

You do such a good job of communicating that your lunch partner buys in and says: "I'd like you to talk to our senior leadership team about this idea. There are implications across our organization that they need to be aware of."

The senior leadership team is comprised of about fifteen people. The group has a fairly similar perspective to your lunch partner about the ideas you're going to present. You'll get forty-five minutes on the agenda, nearly twice the time you had one-on-one.

How many slides will you be tempted to use now? Will you use more or less than you did over lunch? If you believe that a presentation isn't a presentation without slides, you will use more. Many, many more. You'll return to your desk, open your favourite slideware program, click your mouse, and begin.

But enough about you and the fact I haven't yet convinced you that slides should be developed last, if needed, and never first in the content development process. Let's talk about the audience. Specifically, let's talk about your lunch partner and examine how he or she processes information.

Does the way your lunch partner listens to your ideas suddenly change from when you talked over lunch, to when he or she is part of a small group listening to the same person talk about the same concept with the same expected outcome? No. Do the other people in the room absorb your ideas in a radically different manner than that of your lunch partner? Absolutely not.

The tank, bucket and trough are in exactly the same configuration for your lunch partner during the group presentation as over lunch. And the tank, bucket and trough are in similar configuration for every other person in the room. However, instead of having a conversation in which you are focused on whether your partner is filling one bucket at a time, you changed. You combined written and spoken information. You may have asked the group to save their questions until the end, instead of being answered along the way. And, if you're like the vast majority of presenters today, there wasn't a pause anywhere to be found during your presentation.

But you shouldn't change. To achieve the same outcome with the group that you achieved one-on-one, you should have a very similar conversation with the group that you had over lunch. It is the best possible way to help them absorb, understand and apply your ideas.

During lunch, it was your job to inform and persuade an audience of one. If you were enthusiastic about the idea, the words came tumbling out; the rate of word delivery was rapid.

But there were many pauses. You paused to think before speaking. We all do in conversation. And, after conveying each idea, you watched your lunch partner carefully, looking for nods and listening for "uh-huhs" that signal the bucket has been emptied into long-term memory and is ready to be filled again.

If your lunch partner looked puzzled at any point, you probably backtracked, sidetracked or stopped. You may have paused to ask if she or he had any questions. You didn't tell your lunch partner to save her or his questions until the end.

The communication was two-way and direct. It was receiver-driven and adhered to the principle of less is more. You were filling the trough, one bucket at a time.

Before we can go much further in our discussion, we need to first come to a common understanding of the relative size of the bucket that represents working memory. How large is it? How small is it? How many words before ideas spill out and are lost? For someone trying to absorb new or complex information, working memory can hold as little as five or six words before it needs to interact with long-term memory. For information that is familiar, working memory can hold up to twenty words. But make no mistake, even with familiar information, twenty words is the maximum. One bucket must be emptied before the next can be filled if anything is to be retained.

During my training programs, I use a modified version of the broken telephone game to demonstrate how small working memory can be. I position four or five volunteers in different parts of the room. I whisper a phrase into the first person's ear. That person walks over to the second person and whispers the phrase into his or her ear, and so on. The last person repeats the phrase out loud. I use a stopwatch to determine how long it takes for the phrase to go from first person to last. Time is precious. Every presentation has a time limit.

The first phrase I use is "Mary had a little lamb." In the vast majority of the thousands of times I've conducted this exercise, the last person accurately repeats the phrase. Because we already have a place in long-term memory occupied by Mary and her lamb, it takes very little time to process that idea.

For the second round, I use a six-word phrase that I tell participants in advance bears no resemblance to Mary or her lamb. Their goal is to move the second phrase through the same series of steps and repeat it accurately in the same amount of time. The second phrase I use is "Pentium chips operate with titanium co-processors."

During the thousands of times I've conducted this exercise, the phrase has come out perfectly only once or twice. Once was with a group of IT managers, who are obviously familiar with pentium, chips, titanium and processors. While they got the phrase right, it took more than twice as long to go through the chain as Mary and her lamb. The words were familiar, but their arrangement was not. The more complex or unfamiliar the idea, the longer the time needed to process it.

The broken telephone game demonstrates that working memory can be overloaded by six words. On the other side of the spectrum, working memory can hold a maximum of twenty words. If you wish to test this, have someone read a sentence of about twenty words to you at a conversational speed without pausing. When they're done, repeat back what they just said.

When my partner and I first tried this, I couldn't resist making the challenge a bit more difficult. I picked up her credit card statement and said: "Previous changes to cash advance fees and any points reward redemption requirements are described in your February statement."

When I asked her to repeat the information back, she mumbled something about fees and points. Working memory was overloaded; virtually nothing made it to long-term memory. Then I broke the original sentence into three parts to allow working memory an opportunity to interact with long-term memory: "Previous changes to cash advance fees. And any points redemption requirements. Are described in your February statement."

This time, after saying each short piece of information, I allowed her a moment to absorb it before saying the next. Even though we knew it wasn't a fair test because she had heard the information once, she got it right. So we tried another one: "The estimate of the time it will take to pay the new balance. Shown on this statement. Through minimum payments. Is two years, three months." That one she got right the first try.

Working memory operates in a range that can be as small as a few words but does not exceed twenty, even with familiar information. During any presentation, the audience needs silence, and lots of it, to fill each bucket and empty it into long-term memory before being ready to fill again. To feed this process, you should provide your audience with one idea at one time between pauses of significant length. If you don't pause, you force listeners to a choice. They can process what you've just said, thereby missing what you're saying now. Or they can continue to listen to what you're saying now—figuratively dumping the bucket's previous contents onto the ground before filling it again. They cannot do both.

The true paradox of filling the bucket is that less is more. The less you say, the more your audience retains. And there is significant research around this concept in the health care industry related to informed consent. Health care providers have technical expertise, but patients and/or their families ultimately make the final decision on treatment. However, as the debate goes, without understanding the technical aspects of a disease, illness or injury, can patients and their families really make informed decisions?

They can, but research has shown that less is more. The less the health care provider attempts to fully educate the patient about the technical aspects of what ails him or her, the more the patient actually understands. Research also indicates a direct relationship between the number of questions asked by the patient and/ or family per minute during the exchange and the likelihood of better understanding. More questions per minute equals better understanding and improved informed consent.

Years ago, I tested this concept during an engagement in the health care industry. My colleague and I were preparing a presentation to a national paediatric society. The purpose of our presentation was to help physicians communicate the importance of vaccination of teenage daughters for the human pappillomavirus (HPV). How could physicians best help families make informed decisions?

As part of the presentation, and to demonstrate the before and after of an exchange between physician and patient(s), we set up a clinical scenario to video record a mother and her thirteen-year-old daughter during a regular visit to the doctor. The physician broached the topic of HPV vaccination. His goal was to educate them on its value so they could make an informed decision.

Generally, a physician has about five minutes to do this. In the scenario we developed, the physician introduced the topic in two or three minutes. Because he wanted them to be informed, he tried to give them as much information as possible, pausing significantly less than he does in conversation. He dumped the data. During the next two-and-a-half minutes, he answered four or five questions. Simple math tells us his answers were twenty to thirty seconds in length, even to closed questions requiring a simple "yes" or "no" as the answer (with which, as we'll discuss in the next chapter, a single word as the answer can be absolutely acceptable). He told me later that he wants to educate his patients, so he tries to provide as much information as possible within a short time frame. To conclude the first portion of the scenario, we recorded the mother saying she would discuss the concept with the other parent over dinner that night.

After the first round of video recording, everyone took a break. The group chatted among themselves while I took the physician off to one side for about forty-five minutes.

He and I went through a few exercises, then we brought the mother and daughter back in and asked what they remembered about what they had heard less than an hour before. The physician was surprised at how little they retained. There's no way they could have had an informed discussion with another parent over dinner. They couldn't have done so less than an hour later. The physician's attempt to fit more information into a small time frame led to less understanding.

We went through the process a second time. After a sentence or two to re-introduce the topic, mother and daughter started asking questions. They asked nine or ten questions in less than one-and-one-half minutes. The physician felt his answers were too short. From his perspective, he felt he didn't tell them anything. However, as he and I discussed, the mother and daughter got to ask questions that were important to their ability to understand, which only they can truly know.

We broke for lunch. An hour or so later, we brought the mother and daughter back in and asked them what they remembered from the second approach. The difference in their understanding was amazing, even though we all agreed it wasn't a fair test since they had already heard the information once. But they could easily have had an informed discussion with the other parent over dinner.

On camera, I asked the physician what he thought, which he allowed us to play during our presentation at the conference.

"My own feeling is that I like to explain and go into more detail," he replied. "But afterwards, seeing how they responded to the information they had gathered, they seemed to get more with less information from me. This was very interesting and very revealing to me.

"I can feel more confident not going into a lot of detail. I always thought that if I didn't give enough information, I was being derelict in my duties. But if I see them retaining more information, then perhaps that's the way to go."

To effectively fill the bucket, remember that less is always more. The less you say, the more they will ultimately remember.

There is a basic cycle that occurs during relaxed conversation. This cycle, which almost all of us unconsciously follow in everyday conversation, enables speakers to do two things. They can effectively fill listeners' buckets one at a time. And they can allow listeners to empty one bucket at a time in long-term memory before returning to fill the next. The cycle has four steps: I think; I talk; they think; I watch and listen.

The cycle begins when the speaker thinks about what he or she is going to say. In daily life, thinking before talking is a good idea. During presentations, it is critical. This is the first pause. As difficult as it is during presentations, with adrenaline coursing through your veins, take the time to pause for a second or two (or more, if needed) to think about each idea before you say it. Once the idea is formed, in silence, send that idea to the audience. If you're enthusiastic about your ideas, your words will come tumbling out.

This brings us to an important point. There are two elements of pace in effective presentations: rate-of-word-delivery and rate of ideas. The best pace? Get the words out quickly. But pause between ideas.

People are often given advice to slow down when delivering a presentation. But ... the ... way ... they ... often ... interpret ... this ... advice ... is ... to ... slow ... down ... their ... rate ... of ... word ... delivery, and drone on in a monotone. Do not slow down your rate of word delivery. Get the words out quickly if you wish to be conversational. But pause between ideas to allow listeners to absorb.

After you've expressed an idea—a maximum of twenty words—stop talking. Keep your head up. Watch and listen for their reaction. Allow the listener(s) to absorb what was just said, to empty the bucket into the trough and be ready to fill it again. Once there's a nod or "uh-huh" to signal that the bucket is ready to be filled again, think to form your next idea. And repeat the process.

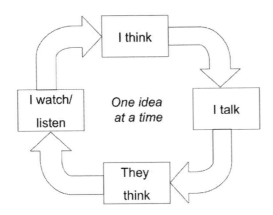

If you watch conversations, you'll discover that this cycle occurs one idea at a time—less than twenty words at a time—during effective exchanges. When you're in the audience during in-person and online presentations after you've read this book, you'll be shocked at how many are non-stop streams of information during which pauses can be ten, twenty or thirty minutes apart. I have absolutely no doubt that the best and most memorable presentations you've ever attended have followed this cycle.

The notes you developed from your basic presentation framework will help emulate conversation. Each note should be a balance between a written script (speech) and no notes (ad-lib, off-the-cuff or memorization) that represents up to twenty words that actually come out of your mouth. As we examined earlier, notes are six to ten word reminders of each idea, similar to the presentation about the framework we developed in the last chapter.

To deliver a note, glance down quickly to grasp it, then look up. With your head up, pause. The first pause does not begin until you lift your head to think, so the down-and-up should be as quick as possible. Use that pause to think, to translate the note into a single full idea, which represents a maximum of twenty words that will come out of your mouth. But don't say anything until that idea is firmly fixed in your mind. Once you've thought it through, express it at your normal rate of word delivery—which is generally as quickly as you can get the words out of your mouth.

After you've expressed the thought, keep your head up and scan the audience for a second or two to see if they've absorbed the idea. This is the second pause.

It's the only point at which eye contact with the audience is necessary or desirable. In that pause, while glancing around, you're asking yourself: Do they understand? Are they ready for more? The audience needs time to think about each idea if they are going to engage with the unfolding of your ideas.

A strong set of notes will help you explain ideas in the simplest possible terms, while adhering to the principle of less is more. If you give your audience time to think, they'll take each idea and add their own level of sophistication. This is the beginning of engagement. It helps them personalize your ideas in a way that makes those ideas directly relevant to who they are as human beings.

Silence is golden during presentations. And there are two types of silence. One is for you to think before talking. This silence—the first pause—ends when you start talking. The second begins when you pause after you've expressed your thought, when you give the audience the opportunity to absorb what you just said. It ends when you drop your head to retrieve your next note.

During your presentations, you're not there to prove you can talk non-stop. You're there to provide information for people to think about and apply to their personal circumstances. But if you wish to capitalize on the opportunity to talk to them, you have to provide them with a bit of silence every twenty words or so. Pause frequently and consistently to allow them to process your ideas.

If you lose your place or your audience, pause. If it's you who's lost, the pause allows you to think about where you are, where you're going and what you need to say to get there. If your audience is lost, the pause will help them find their way back so they can listen to your ideas again and fill one bucket at a time. This gives them the opportunity to remember your ideas long after both you and they have left the room.

TOP UP THE TROUGH

Most of us would never start a text conversation with someone by typing: "I'm going to send fifteen screens of information. When I'm done sending, please feel free to ask questions." If I started a text conversation like that with one of my kids, they would think the old man has finally lost it. If I started an in-person conversation with one of them like that, they'd probably pull out their smartphone, ignore me, and let me drone on.

However, this is precisely the approach taken during the vast majority of presentations delivered every day. Somehow, when we finally get the opportunity to bring people together (whether in person or via video link), it's acceptable for the person delivering the presentation to ask the audience to save questions until all information has first been sent. And, let's face it, the audience is lucky if it's only fifteen screens.

The simplest way to breathe life into modern presentations is to create an equal, engaging partnership with the audience by encouraging and answering their questions. Give them a chance to probe your ideas. The simple exercise of them asking questions helps cement those ideas into part of who they are. When that happens, they'll be applying those ideas long after you and they have left the room.

In a partnership, half the available time belongs to you, and half the time belongs to them. The ability to ask questions enables them to fill in gaps that you can never conceivably consider unless, of course, you can read minds, which you can't. They will never have your level of understanding about your subject. But you will never know what they know, nor will you know what they don't know, without some form of participation from them.

For more than twenty years, I have asked participants at workshops and seminars whether questions should be encouraged throughout a presentation, or saved until the end. Increasingly, people have said that questions should be saved to the end.

"Why do you prefer that?" I ask.

"Because the presentation will get off track," they reply.

"But who gets off track?" I ask. "The person asking? Or the person answering?"

After a brief discussion, it doesn't take long before we all realize that the person answering most often gets off track. The answers are long and convoluted. She or he often answers dozens of questions that weren't asked. Sometimes this is interesting to the audience. The vast majority of the time it isn't.

If you truly wish to set yourself and your ideas apart—if you're looking to create an environment in which communication flourishes—questions from the audience are essential. They should be encouraged and answered whenever and wherever possible.

And it's almost always possible. The minimum standard should be to save at least one-third of the time for questions at the end. Minimum. The next step up is to answer questions at the end of each section of the presentation. The ideal scenario is when questions are encouraged and answered throughout the presentation.

The moderator of a webinar can bring questions to the presenter, either throughout the presentation or, as a minimum, at the end of each section. Microphones can be positioned throughout a room during larger presentations. However, if there are twenty-five people or fewer in attendance, there is no reason for not answering questions from start to finish. In fact, with insights from this chapter and a little practice, it should be more than possible to answer questions throughout your presentation with audiences of fifty participants or more. I have done it with more than three hundred people in the room, while completing my presentation and finishing on time.

The exchange of ideas is the true value of bringing people together—whether during in-person presentations or through technology like video calls, webinars and teleseminars. Understanding flourishes when audiences have the opportunity to probe ideas, especially if the person answering understands the value of clear, succinct answers.

D uring the past twenty-five years, however, I have come to the conclusion that the skill of answering questions is perhaps the least-developed skill in human interpersonal communication. We all know someone who we're reluctant to ask "how are you today?" because it will be tomorrow or the next day by the time they get around to telling us how they were on what used to be today.

These people don't wake up in the morning wondering how many others they can bore to death. They believe they're being helpful. And, in truth, long answers are often an attempt to help others understand. But the best way to help others is not to teach them by providing long, rambling answers. Instead, let them teach themselves with clear, concise answers. Answer as many questions as possible within the allotted time and they will better understand and retain your ideas.

It isn't easy. Even I have to be vigilant in my ability to be clear and concise and I, of all people, should know better. I teach this concept every day. Yet I still find there are times when I'll be prattling on with an answer that sounds good to me, but when I draw a breath and look around, I realize that nobody's listening. I've bored them or confused them, or both.

Long answers are almost never two-way or receiver-driven. They do not adhere to the principle of less is more. And, more often than not, they confuse the audience. Clear, concise answers achieve the opposite.

A number of years ago, I was providing presentation training to a small group of institutional money managers, who managed billions in pension assets between them. One of the participants, a fixed income manager, was impressive even by this group's standards. That night I told my partner his shoes were probably worth more than our car.

"In my experience," he told me during the workshop, "short answers are not appropriate. My clients like to know that I know what I'm talking about. And I have to educate them."

"No problem," I said. "We'll take a look at that when we get there."

When he later delivered his presentation while being video recorded, I asked a question that was appropriate to his topic: "Given that you say you don't make bets on duration, isn't the way you work the yield curve similar to a bet on duration?"

It's a closed question, requiring yes or no as the answer. In these situations, it's perfectly acceptable to answer "yes" or "no" and stop talking, or add a few words after the answer. In this specific case, the answer was no. "No, it's not like a bet on duration."

But he couldn't help himself. He talked for nearly four minutes. Nonstop. When we reviewed the video recording of his presentation, I let all four minutes play uninterrupted. He later told me it was the longest four minutes of his life. When I gently interrupted him on the recording to ask another question, I paused the playback and turned to him. "Unlike your clients, I can calculate duration. You have less need to educate me, yet I have no idea what you're talking about right now."

He looked rather sheepish as he replied. "If you could understand, I'd be really impressed. I'm watching me and I've confused myself."

He became a disciple of shorter answers on his way to bigger and better things. Years later, he brought me in to work with one of his portfolio managers. It was a delicate engagement; egos were involved.

We went for coffee to discuss the assignment. After a quick recap, he let me ask questions. The situation was indeed delicate. But in ten or fifteen minutes, during which I literally asked dozens of questions, we developed a plan that ended up working very well.

He was so good at answering questions that even I didn't pick up on it until we were almost done. When he saw in my eyes that I was delighted with his communication skills, he smiled and said: "You taught me well." It was one of the most rewarding moments of my career.

To improve your ability to answer questions, keep three words in mind: pause-answer-stop. Pause, answer the question asked (and *only* the question asked), and stop talking. If you can do this, your friends will thank you. Your family will thank you. Your colleagues will thank you. Your staff will thank you. Your bosses and clients will thank you. And whenever you deliver a presentation, your audiences will thank you. Pause-answer-stop is the key to answering questions in a way that facilitates communication and enhances understanding.

When my partner and I decided to put ceramic tile through our entranceway and kitchen, we were undecided about whether to do the job ourselves or hire a contractor. To do some research, I went to our local home improvement store. I had the good fortune of encountering a very confident young man who had obviously installed a lot of ceramic tile. I know he was confident because he didn't feel compelled to talk endlessly whenever I asked him a question. In fact, he simply answered each question I asked and stopped talking, waiting patiently for the next question to be asked.

During the fifteen or twenty minutes that we chatted, I probably asked close to a hundred questions. Our daughter was with me, and as we were walking out of the store she remarked: "Dad, that was amazing. I can't believe how much I learned. Even I know what needs to be done to install tiles. You asked great questions."

Actually, I didn't ask great questions. I was simply given the opportunity to ask a lot of questions to teach myself—which occurred because the person answering paused, answered the question, and stopped talking.

The skill of answering questions is the art of matching the clear, concise answer directly to the question asked. This should be the goal whenever you're answering questions in your personal or professional life. And pause-answer-stop is the key to getting there.

Whenever an answer extends for more than ten words, you're making assumptions about what's important to whoever asked the question. Beyond twenty seconds, you increase the probability that people have stopped listening. If all answers extend beyond twenty seconds, don't be surprised if they simply quit asking.

As we'll discuss in a moment, the vast majority of questions can be answered in ten words or less. Virtually every question on the planet can be answered in twenty seconds or less.

While answering questions, resist the temptation to create a decision tree in your head. In other words, don't engage in a mental exercise of: "If I answer this with yes, he or she will ask that. Then if I answer that ..."

When you create a decision tree, you listen less effectively. Answers become imprecise. They become longer. As such, they become widely open to interpretation, so they're often interpreted along a wide spectrum. This is counter-productive if your goal is to communicate effectively. Precise, succinct answers are the key to building understanding.

W henever you're asked a question in your personal or professional life, pause before answering. First of all, it's polite. Pausing enables you to provide short answers without seeming to be rude or abrupt. If you shoot back a yes or no without pausing, you create a completely different perception than pausing, considering the question, and responding with "yes" or "no."

Pausing gives you time to think. You can ensure you understand the question. Always ask for clarification if you don't. Then pause and provide the best possible answer, which is almost always the shortest possible answer.

You look thoughtful and confident when you pause. People in control of themselves and their environment take time to compose themselves. Contrast this with those who blurt out answers and keep talking. If you've ever conducted a job interview with someone young and inexperienced, you know exactly what I'm talking about.

By pausing, you compliment the questioner. The question required time to think, ergo it was a good question. This brings us to another point. You cannot buy time to think by telling someone they asked a good question. If you need time to think (and we almost always do), take it. In silence.

Pausing before answering enables you to control emotion during situations in which there is real or perceived hostility. If you're ever participated in a question-and-answer exchange where emotions run high, you know the value of pausing, or the risks associated with not pausing.

Pausing helps establish a pattern in which difficult questions don't stand out. If someone asks a series of questions that you answer without pausing, difficult questions become obvious because it's the first time you pause. If you've established a pattern of pausing throughout, difficult questions are not as obvious. This provides a level of protection.

Finally, you become a better listener by pausing. As we've discussed, human beings cannot think and listen at the same time. If you feel the need to answer the question as soon as it's asked, you're already thinking of the answer while the person is still asking. Establishing a pattern of pausing before answering enables you to separate listening from thinking, which enhances your listening skills.

How long should you pause? It depends. Pause at least a second or so to ensure that you're polite and complimentary and to prevent difficult questions from being obvious. However, if you need more time to think, take it. If you start talking before you're ready, your answers will be longer, less precise and ultimately less supportive of the goals you're attempting to achieve.

Answer the question that was asked, and only the question asked. People who ask a question are seeking one thing: *the* answer. They don't want another speech or presentation. They're not seeking answers to questions yet unasked. They're simply seeking the answer to the question.

In your daily life, when people ask "What time is it?," you don't tell them you're glad they asked that question or say "that's a good question." You don't provide them with background information related to your watch, then go into a lengthy description of that background. You simply look at your watch and answer the question.

During your presentations, if the answer is "yes," people will want to hear it. The same applies if the answer is "no," "possibly," "absolutely," "eventually," "unlikely," or "only under certain circumstances." How much more they want or need to hear will surprise you when you begin examining the question-and-answer process from the receiver's perspective—which, truly, is the only perspective that counts. As a general statement, the person asking almost always wants less information than the person answering feels compelled to provide.

If the answer to the question is "under certain circumstances," tell them so and stop. If they're interested in the circumstances, they'll ask. If not, move on. Trust me. If people believe that answering their questions is important to you and your answers are succinct, they'll ask more questions if they're remotely interested.

If answers are lengthy, audiences simply stop asking questions. I've witnessed this hundreds of times at presentations, but one of the more amusing examples occurred when I was providing presentation training to rookie advisors at a brokerage firm.

My portion of the agenda was scheduled for an evening and subsequent full day. It was a regular gig, and my normal habit was to arrive for the catered dinner, then conduct the evening session from 6:30 to 8:30 p.m. On one occasion, I arrived an hour before dinner, so I decided to quietly slip into the back of the room to watch the consultant in the time slot ahead of me.

He was talking about fixed income. With about twenty minutes remaining before the dinner break, one of the participants asked a closed question that technically required "yes" or "no" as the answer. The consultant told the group he was going to give them the short answer, so I thought I'd time him. Fourteen minutes later, he stopped for a breath and asked: "Are there any more questions?"

The person who originally asked the question had put his feet up on the desk to read the newspaper, with it between him and the person answering. Almost everyone else was checking e-mail at the computer terminals in front of them. Not a soul was listening. When he finally stopped to ask if there were any additional questions, everyone snapped up their heads and started glancing around the room. We could all smell the inviting aroma of the catered buffet that was waiting for us just outside the training room door. The message they were sending each other was clear, if unspoken: "Don't you dare ask another question."

There are three acceptable answers to every question you can be asked:

- Yes, I have the answer and here it is.

- No, I don't have the answer but I'll get it for you.

- Yes, I do have the answer but I cannot provide it to you.

There are six or seven very specific cases in which you would use the third response—for example, if providing the answer would divulge sensitive competitive information, break client confidentiality or breach securities legislation. For example, "I cannot answer that question because next-of-kin haven't been notified" or "I cannot answer that question for reasons related to national security." In every other case, the first two answers apply. Either you have the answer and you'll provide it, or you don't have it and you'll get it.

There are situations in which you might get asked a number of questions at once. For example, someone might ask: "Are you sure you should keep your answers short? What if the question requires a lengthy answer? What if people want to know more?" By pausing, you can sort through these multiple questions before answering them. You may even confirm one or more questions before answering. You might respond by saying: "Let me see if I understand your questions. Should we always keep our answer short? Absolutely. What if the question requires a lengthy answer? Most questions can be answered in ten words or less. If people want to know more, they'll ask more questions."

Be careful with loaded questions, or questions that are based on an incorrect assumption. For example, someone may ask: "You've said this software platform will not be ready on time, so how critical is it that we get you the information by next Friday?" If the initial premise of this question is incorrect, you must remove it or clarify the misperception before answering. A possible reply could be: "I didn't say the software won't be ready on time. We're currently a bit behind schedule. Getting information by Friday will put us back on schedule."

If you're unsure what someone is asking, don't guess. Check with them, or rephrase the question and ask: "Was that what you were asking?" Once you get confirmation that it was, pause while you form an appropriate answer, answer the question, and stop talking.

Stop talking as soon as you've answered the question. This is the hardest challenge of face-to-face communication—whether one-on-one or with groups. Nothing is more difficult. However, the value it brings to the communication process is nothing short of amazing. If the audience wants more, they'll ask, especially if you create an environment in which they feel comfortable asking.

Once you've answered the question, even if the answer is "yes" or "no," stop talking. If you see a puzzled expression, stop. If you see that the other person is forming or thinking about a question, stop. When in doubt, stop. Clarify if necessary, but answer and stop. Let them teach themselves about your ideas by participating in an exchange that facilitates more questions, not less.

As a training tool, I often introduce a slightly tongue-in-cheek guideline I call "the ten-pushup rule" to help people realize the value of clear, concise answers. The rule is quite simple. The person answering gets a maximum of ten words with which to answer any question. For every word over ten, she or he is required to do ten pushups per word at the end of the exchange.

The ten-pushup rule highlights the value of succinct answers. I never make people do the pushups, and only one person ever has actually done them. He was a particularly fit CEO who had been sitting too long and dropped to do fifty when we reviewed a recording of questions I asked during training. He was disappointed that his answer was fifteen words when a simple "yes" or "no" would have sufficed. Five words over ten equals fifty pushups. It was actually quite impressive.

The ten-pushup rule is an amazing tool. I've witnessed its positive impact thousands of times. When someone has a word limit on answers, her or his behaviour immediately changes. The first thing that happens is the person listens more carefully to the question asked.

Next, the person answering communicates more effectively. With a limit on answer length, he or she has no choice but to exactly and precisely answer the question that was asked. This puts the audience first.

The person answering doesn't have time to anticipate where questions are going. With a limit on answer length, he or she deals with one question at a time. This is truly the skill of answering questions effectively: matching the precise answer to the exact question asked.

Limiting the length of your answers will feel unnatural. Absolutely. But I have been teaching clients for more than twenty-five years that they should embrace that feeling. If you feel the answer was too short for you, it was probably perfect for whoever asked. If it was a complete answer, it was probably a bit long for those listening. If it was a full and complete answer with just the right amount of important background information, trust me. They quit listening long ago.

The ten-pushup rule has never failed to improve someone's ability to communicate effectively. One example, however, stands out as particularly striking, because it demonstrated the understanding that short answers can generate.

I was providing a half-day of introductory media training to about a dozen senior managers of a municipality. With a group that large during such a short time, there's not much opportunity to conduct practice media interviews. However, within the limited time available, I wanted to make the point that short answers are critical to helping people understand—not just during exchanges with print journalists, but in everyday life.

So I made an unusual request. I asked for a volunteer, but with specific requirements. I said I wanted someone who probably lies or changes the subject if asked at a party what he or she does for a living. Everyone looked puzzled, so I clarified. I said I needed the one person in the room who, even though he or she has worked with others in the room for years, has a job no one really understands. At that point, everyone pointed to one person: the municipality's senior risk manager.

With some prompting from his peers, he came to the front of the room and sat down for his recorded interview. I began by asking him about his job and how he added value to the municipality. During four minutes, I only managed to ask three or four questions. He wanted to educate us about his job, especially since the group had clearly said they didn't understand what he did, so his answers were long. I let him talk.

I stopped recording and asked how he thought he had done. "I think really well," he said. "I managed to get my points across." However, from his colleagues' expressions, I could tell they didn't understand any more after the exchange than they did before.

Then I introduced the ten-pushup rule. I told him we would keep track of the number of words he used per answer—we were recording the exchange, so it would be easy—and that for each word over ten, he would be asked to complete ten pushups per word at the end of the interview. I jokingly told him that he will either be brief or he will become fit.

I started recording again and asked him about his job. The change in his demeanour was fascinating. He listened more carefully to what I was asking. He paused to think, simply answered the question, and stopped talking. At the end of about three to four minutes, during which I asked two to three dozen questions, I stopped recording and thanked him for his participation. He got up, and all the way back to his seat grumbled about how the second interview was terrible. He felt he didn't get a chance to tell me anything.

However, the reaction from the group made me smile. The best way to describe it is stunned silence. You could have heard a pin drop.

When he sat down, the person beside him turned to him and said: "You and I have been close friends for five or six years, right? For the first time, I actually understand what you do for a living." I played the first and second interviews without interruption. When the risk manager watched the before and after versions, the look on his face showed that he clearly agreed.

Short answers are effective in helping people understand. It is the place where the presenter's knowledge meets the audience's need to understand. If handled properly, this is when communication is extremely powerful.

Granted, if a relatively simple concept is explained during a five-minute project update, people may not need to ask many questions to improve their understanding. However, if the concept is even remotely complex, or if there's anything out of the ordinary in that update, people need to ask. Simply marching through information does not guarantee understanding.

And that raises another important point. If someone asks a question about something you plan to cover later during the presentation, what do you do? Should you encourage the person to hold the question until you get to that section?

Let's examine that from the perspective of what we've already discussed. People cannot listen and think at the same time. By asking the person to hold onto a question, you are actually asking them to keep thinking about that question and stop listening.

When asked a question on a subject you're going to cover later, answer the question in the fewest words possible. If the person has follow-up questions, answer those the same way. If you answer five or six questions concisely, you won't get off track because the exercise should take less than a minute, and will certainly take less than two. When you cover the topic later, your content will simply reinforce your earlier answers.

Some people are okay with answering questions one-on-one, but resist when the audience gets even marginally larger (i.e. a group of ten or twelve). Yes, audience size can have an impact. There may be technical issues to be addressed with audiences of more than fifty people. Whoever's asking the question needs to be heard by all, as does whoever's answering. But there is absolutely no reason for saving questions to the end of a presentation with twenty-five people or fewer in the audience.

By asking questions, audiences can probe the specific areas of your knowledge important to their need to understand. This is something you can never predict; it is something only they can determine. Having their questions answered is engaging. It enables the audience to make informed decisions about your ideas—to either apply the information you're presenting or take action on it.

Pause. Answer. Stop. It is the key to helping people understand your ideas, and potentially applying or taking action on those ideas after your presentation concludes.

TAP THE POTENTIAL

When you strip it to its core component, tapping the potential of the presentation medium boils down to engagement. How engaged was the audience with what was said? Did they have a chance to process ideas? Were they interested enough to ask questions? How many did they ask? How likely are they to apply or take action on what was presented? Will they be able to later talk to others about what they think they understood?

I have come to the conclusion that engagement operates along a continuum. At one end there is the bare minimum, which is to engage working memory and long-term memory in a meaningful way. If this doesn't happen, nothing else matters. At the other end of the engagement spectrum, we have the ability of those attending presentations being able to explain the ideas to others.

Engagement has to be carefully and properly nurtured. The argument has often been made that the greater the stimulus thrown at the audience, the greater the level of engagement. That's one of the reasons for using slides and why we often see advertisements for workshops designed to teach participants how to "create engaging slides." But as we've discussed, any form of reading and listening at the same time overloads working memory. This reduces engagement. People don't engage with slides. They engage with other human beings who have something meaningful to say, and who say it in a memorable way.

I was once hired by a pharmaceutical company to deliver a one-and-one-half hour presentation to a group of urologists who had gathered to put the finishing touches on a continuing medical education program that was being rolled out across the country. My role was to talk to them about how they could communicate their knowledge when they later fanned out to conduct workshops.

The meeting took place at a resort in a remote location. I arrived the evening before and had an early night. I awoke early and decided to go for breakfast and watch the presentation that preceded my talk.

I was delighted that I did. One of the urologists stood at the front of the room and took approximately thirty of his peers through the information they would later be asked to present. He was a brilliant communicator. He didn't show a single slide. He showed two short videos (one of which, a laser procedure inside a urethra, I could have lived my entire life without seeing). He created a conversation with his colleagues that, in forty-five minutes, provided incredible insight. He answered close to a hundred questions. He put into practice virtually everything we've talked about here. It was a case study in communication effectiveness. Everyone was engaged.

During the short break after his talk, there was a buzz in the room. People were talking in small groups. Everyone was commenting on how how much they learned and how the session was one of the best—if not *the* best—they had ever attended. After a short break, they broke into groups to spend an hour putting the finishing touches on the slides they would later use in their own workshops.

This exercise took longer than anticipated. No surprise there. When they reconvened at 11:30 a.m., I had about half an hour before we had to break for lunch so people could board buses back to the city and catch flights home. My presentation couldn't run late. I could have given a short version of my talk, but I didn't. After all, I thought, I had been hired to help them understand how to communicate effectively to achieve the outcomes they're seeking, and we had all witnessed the gold standard that very morning.

I focused their attention on the earlier presentation their colleague delivered. To a person, they agreed it was brilliant. Everyone learned a lot. I asked how many slides their colleague used. This caught them by surprise. It took a minute or two before they realized he hadn't used any, which he verified (he was in the room). Interestingly, until I pointed it out, nobody even realized that he hadn't used a single slide. He engaged their minds.

Then I asked if they were going to use the slides they spent the past two-and-a-half hours working on when they delivered their own sessions. When they said yes, I quietly asked: "Why? Wouldn't it be better to do what we all saw earlier and just talk to the audience?" At first there was silence. Then they pushed back.

To say that this evolved into a spirited conversation would be an understatement. Anyone watching would have thought I had refuted the holy grail of urology without a single shred of evidence. "That's the way CME programs are delivered," one physician commented (forgetting again that the earlier session hadn't used any slides). Another told me that CME programs had been delivered that way since speakers actually carried carousels of 35-mm slides from presentation to presentation. (Been there. Done that.) That's the way it's done, and that's the way it has always been done.

Perhaps, I said. But wouldn't it be better to replicate what we had witnessed earlier? If that approach helped this group learn, which they all agreed it did, wouldn't it also benefit other groups?

To close, I said I hoped they would bring a similar analysis to the communication process that they bring to their profession. There's no doubt that communication is an art. But there is a growing body of science around communication.

Simply sending a message isn't enough. Ensuring that information is applied is the key to success. The more the audience thinks about the information presented, the greater the likelihood they will apply it or take action on it. This happens when presentations engage minds, not eyeballs.

B eyond the interaction of working and long-term memory, the next step along the engagement continuum is questions asked by the audience. This is an unerring indicator of engagement. Which audience is more engaged? The audience that asks four or five questions at the end of a fifty-minute march through slides? Or the audience that asks thirty, forty or more questions throughout a sixty-minute exchange? My money's on the latter. The audience that asks more wants to know more. They are engaged.

I have a tool I call the Q-ratio, which provides a simple metric with which to measure relative engagement. In simplest terms, the Q-ratio is the number of questions asked by the audience per minute for the duration of the presentation. To arrive at the ratio, divide the number of questions the audience asks by the number of minutes available for the presentation. It applies only to questions asked by the audience. Rhetorical questions asked by the presenter are not included.

Wherever possible, strive for a Q-ratio of one or higher during presentations. In other words, if you have a one-hour time frame for a presentation (including questions), bring thirty minutes of information and strive to generate sixty-plus questions from the audience. If you have thirty minutes (for which you only bring fifteen minutes of information), strive to generate and answer at least thirty questions. If you're conducting a full-day workshop, you should strive to answer hundreds of questions from participants. And so on.

Is this achievable? Not always, but it should always be the goal.

However, it's fairly easy to demonstrate that a Q-ratio of one is possible in almost any circumstance, as long as answers are concise. To demonstrate this at workshops, I play a game entitled "do you drink coffee?"

I begin by asking the group to focus on one hour as the time frame for a presentation, including questions from the audience. When they agree they have attended or conducted presentations of sixty minutes' length, I write this time frame down as "60" on a flip chart or whiteboard.

Next, I ask them to provide the maximum number of questions they have ever seen asked by the audience and answered by the presenter during a one-hour presentation, whether delivered by them or others. In the thousands of times I've done this, the most common response I get is four to five questions asked by the audience and answered by the presenter during sixty minutes of presentation time.

Think about your own experience. Sixty minutes. Four or five questions. Doesn't sound very engaging, does it?

I then ask the group who should control the direction of the question-and-answer process. Should the person asking have greater influence over its direction? Or the person answering? Invariably, someone picks answering. I then ask that person if he or she minds if I ask a few questions. Once I get permission to proceed, I ask a series of questions that goes something like:

Do you drink coffee?
- Yes

How many cups per day?
- Two or three.

Always two or three?
- Sometimes I might have more, but rarely.

Why would you drink more than three cups of coffee on a particular day?
- I might have an afternoon meeting with a client over a cup of coffee.

Do you also drink coffee on weekends?
- Yes.

If so, how many cups?

- About the same.

How old were you when you started drinking coffee?

- Fifteen or sixteen. Probably some time in high school.

Do you think high school is a little early to start drinking coffee?

- No.

Did you drink coffee at university?

- Yes.

What did you study at university?

- I studied commerce.

At this point, I stop and ask the group if they could have predicted that we were going to arrive at "what did you study at university?" from "do you drink coffee?" None could. Then I ask if I could have predicted it. After a brief discussion, I hand my coffee-drinking subject a piece of paper on which I've previously written "What did you study at university?" and ask them to read it aloud.

I have played this game thousands of times and have always been able to end at "What did you study at university?" (or "What would have studied at university if you'd attended") from "Do you drink coffee?" by asking ten to twelve closed and open-ended questions, generally in a minute or less. Ten questions in one minute equals a Q-ratio of ten.

The coffee exchange demonstrates how many questions can be asked and answered in a short period of time, as long as answers are succinct. It usually takes about a minute to ask ten to fifteen questions in a way that makes each question a natural extension of the last.

Second, the coffee drinking game establishes who should determine the direction of the question-and-answer process. The person asking questions should set the direction if the intent is to enhance engagement, improve decision-making and lead to better understanding. Misunderstandings occur when the person answering assumes she or he knows what's being asked. To clear up misunderstandings, don't assume. Listen to the question being asked. Pause and think of the answer to the question. Answer it and stop talking.

To demonstrate the difference between short and long answers, I repeat the coffee drinker's answers back to the group with something like: "I'm glad you asked whether I drink coffee. Normally I drink two to three cups a day. Sometimes I might have more, but rarely. I might have an afternoon meeting with a client over a cup of coffee. I also drink coffee on weekends. Again, it's about two to three cups.

"I started drinking coffee when I was about fifteen or sixteen years of age. It was sometime in high school. I don't think high school was too early to start drinking coffee. I drank coffee at university. I studied commerce at university, and it was a wonderful foundation on which I've constructed my career.

"Anyone else have a question?"

The group usually gets a chuckle when I repeat back the coffee drinker's clear, concise answers in a long string of information. But when the laughter settles, we have a discussion about whether this is truly unlike the way in which questions are answered during presentations, an in other aspects of people's personal and professional lives. Trust me. It isn't.

At this point, I return to the flip chart on which I wrote "60" as the time frame for presentations and do some simple algebra. The "60" represents the number of minutes in a one-hour presentation. If I can ask ten questions in one minute, the audience can potentially ask "x" questions in thirty minutes (which should be the time available for the audience in a one hour presentation). By cross-multiplying, we discover that "x" equals three hundred questions in sixty minutes, for a Q-ratio of five. Will you ever get there? Not likely. But it makes answering sixty questions in one hour a lot more achievable.

The higher the Q-ratio, the better the engagement. The back-and-forth of the question-and-answer process is an excellent way to facilitate engagement and help the audience make your ideas part of who they are. It should be every presenter's goal to achieve a Q-ratio of one every time people are brought together.

There are a couple of ways to generate questions. The most obvious is to keep asking if the audience has any questions. In any audience of twenty-five or fewer, you should be constantly checking to see if they have questions they'd like to ask. You should do this during your introduction, as early as after you've informed them of what's going to be discussed, how they should apply or take action on your information, and the main topic areas you'll cover.

At that point, I often say: "I don't want you to hold questions until the end. If you have a question at any point, please ask. I'll do my best to answer clearly and concisely.

"In fact, are there any questions so far?"

Every time you ask for questions, stop talking. Pause. Pause for as long as you possibly can, then count another slow ten seconds in your head. If you do this at the end of the introduction and at the end of each section of the presentation, trust me. If they have questions, they'll ask. If they don't, move on.

The most effective way to generate questions is to remove slides from view. Turn off the projector. Audiences are now conditioned to sit quietly and stop talking as soon as slides start. If you observe presentations now (or become aware of your own reaction), you will see and feel this in action. Eyes glaze over and audiences begin to tune out as soon as the projector is turned on or the screen is shared and the presenter is relegated to secondary status.

I have witnessed the phenomenon of turning off the projector many times. One of the more memorable was when I was a speaker at an evening forum for young engineers interested in earning their full professional credentials. I was brought in to talk about how they could improve their communication skills as their careers progressed. I showed a one-minute video that illustrated the importance of separating the written word from the spoken, demonstrated that concept with two charts (separated by blank slides), then shut the projector off and talked about the value of delivering ideas conversationally, even during technical presentations. I had a portable whiteboard I used a few times to illustrate points. I answered at least forty to fifty questions along the way, and finished a few minutes early.

The group took a short break before a speaker from the engineering association delivered a forty-five minute presentation on the steps required to earn full engineering credentials. During the break, she turned on the projector, attached her laptop, and began loading her forty-slide presentation. Watching this, some of the young engineers commented on how many slides they were about to see, based on what they had heard during the previous hour.

The presenter, who had been in the room for that hour, looked a little uncertain, so I walked over and quietly said: "If you need your slides as notes, use them. But shut off the projector." She did shut it off. Shortly after she started her presentation, an interesting thing happened. The group began asking questions. And they didn't just ask questions, they peppered her.

"I've just changed jobs," one person said. "What information do I need from my previous employer? Do I need anything different from my current employer?"

"I've just been laid off," another said. "How will that affect my path to becoming licensed? Can I get an extension if I need it?"

"My supervisor is an engineer in Brazil," a third one pointed out. "Are translation services available?"

On it went. There were even questions from older engineers who acted as mentors and sponsors. They asked questions to gain insight into helping younger engineers succeed. Luckily, she had been paying attention during the section of my presentation on the ten-pushup rule and provided concise answers. She easily answered fifty to sixty questions, which helped the audience match her information to their particular circumstances.

Her slides were designed to take the group through the steps required to achieve certification. Honestly, if the people in the audience didn't already know those steps, they probably shouldn't have been there in the first place. Getting together in person was a valuable opportunity to help them determine how those steps could be applied to a variety of circumstances.

The audience was engaged, and so was I. There is no doubt that everyone who left that room (including me) could have correctly answered questions about the licensing process, or known where to send someone for more information. By answering their questions, she didn't just deliver her presentation. She brought it alive.

A t this point, I'd like take a bit of a step to the side in our discussion of engagement to share an observation I've made during more than twenty-five years of presentation skills training to thousands upon thousands of people. I have never seen anyone improve their skills by turning on a projector. In fact, the opposite has always been true. Whether neophyte or seasoned pro, everyone who has turned off the projector and continued delivering their presentation has enhanced their ability to communicate effectively—to move ideas from tank to trough, one bucket at a time.

Over the years, participants at workshops have challenged my assertion that slide-driven presentations cannot be delivered conversationally, and I've always let them to try to prove me wrong. On the second day of a two-day presentation skills program, for example, I often let people use slides as they've always done, while trying to incorporate the conversational approach we focused on the day before. They deliver four or five minutes of their presentation, then I shut off the projector and ask them to deliver the next four or five minutes without showing slides, but using their slides as notes. Both segments are video recorded.

During playback we watch two or three minutes of each version, and I let everyone judge for themselves. In all the times I've done this exercise, nobody's ability to communicate improved when slides were shown, no matter how much they believed in pausing when they tried. Every time the projector has been turned off, the person's presentation skills have significantly improved.

There may be a variety of reasons for this. There are fewer distractions for both audience and presenter. The audience is focused on what the presenter is saying, not what she or he is showing. I did the before and after exercise once with a client who has a PhD in psychology. In an introspective moment, he said he when slides were showing, it felt as if people weren't listening, so his natural instinct was to talk more, not less.

A few years ago, I incorporated the concept of shutting off the projector into a full-day workshop for about twenty-five emergency physicians from across Toronto. My contact told me that these physicians are often called upon to provide continuing medical education workshops. His goal was to help them improve their skills.

My contact is the head of emergency medicine at a large hospital group in the Toronto area, and a sought-after speaker. His workshops are anticipated, attended and often applauded. We had first worked together twenty-four years before, when I provided training to him and a few of his colleagues. Our relationship continued over the years. He engaged me a number of times to provide workshops to emergency physicians and other health care providers, and we've had lunch a few times. He once told me that he's never learned to use slides.

When he contacted me about conducting this one-day workshop, he had a special request. "I'd like you to take people through your early process, where you have them go through your 'drill' in the morning and learn about your content models, but I'd like to have them bring presentations to deliver in the afternoon and get your feedback."

"But Eric," I countered (his name is also Eric), "we both know that they'll bring their presentations in PowerPoint. How can I have them realize the value of conversational presentations when they bring slides?"

"I don't know," he replied. "But I'm sure you'll figure it out before we get together in a few weeks."

I'd be lying if I said I didn't lose sleep over this one. But I came up with a plan. I took the group through my exercises and drills in the morning, and introduced the basic presentation framework and the use of notes just before lunch.

During lunch, I worked with one physician to change the presentation he had brought on managing patients who present with symptoms of severe alcoholism. We set the slides he brought aside and started with the framework. I then helped him develop five minutes of notes (the outline format we talked about earlier). The entire exercise took less than thirty minutes. When we were done he said "I don't think I need slides, do you?"

After lunch, half of the participants stayed with me and half went to a breakout room with my client and my assistant. Presentations in both rooms were video recorded.

Our approach was simple. We had each person deliver three or four minutes of their presentation using slides, then turned off the projector. For the next three or four minutes they used their slides as notes, and delivered their notes using the cycle we talked about earlier: I think; I talk; they think; I watch and listen. We then played back about two minutes from each version so the person (and the group) could see the difference.

It is something I should have implemented a long, long time ago. In every case, the presenter's ability to communicate improved. There were no exceptions. Everyone strengthened their ability to help the audience move ideas from tank to trough, one bucket at a time.

Near the end of the day, both groups reconvened in one room. The physician I worked with during lunch delivered his five-minute presentation on patients presenting with symptoms of severe alcoholism. It was a real-time exercise, as it was an issue at every hospital. What happened next was amazing.

He encouraged questions from the audience. He got them, and the exchange evolved into a problem-solving process. They developed a protocol that was flexible enough to address the concerns of individual hospitals, yet met the needs of all. It was an exercise in communication effectiveness and group problem-solving, and the protocol was adopted by emergency departments across the region.

The audience was engaged. They were taking his ideas and comparing them to the specific challenges at their emergency department. They asked questions. And they contributed insights. When a group of like-minded professionals have a chance to interact, good things happen.

At the end of the day, one of the physicians came up to me and said: "I was very skeptical when I learned you don't believe in using slides. But watching every one of us improve was an incredible learning experience. I want you to know that I will never again develop my content with PowerPoint, and that if I ever use a slide again, it will only be when and where absolutely necessary."

The next step along the engagement continuum is action. With informative presentations, the action is to apply the information. With persuasive presentations, the emphasis is on behaviour—to vote, to buy, to sell, to schedule a follow-up meeting, to hire. The question here is simple: Do slides support action or hinder it? I have no doubt it's the latter.

Nearly twenty years ago, after I finished delivering a presentation to a group of financial services professionals on the west coast, one of the participants approached me and said: "I was fascinated by the part of your presentation where you talked about slides getting in the way of sales results. My business partner and I proved that to ourselves without a doubt."

He told me that he and his partner have built a significant portion of their business through financial seminars. At the time we spoke, they had delivered presentations and/or seminars once or twice a week for years. They had the process down to a science and were very successful. (The conference at which I spoke was sponsored by a life insurance company that had only invited top tier producers to attend.)

They kept their seminar topics current and presented the information themselves. They carefully selected and segmented their prospects. They knew how many people their marketing assistants needed to contact to fill each seminar. Each seminar was kept to fewer than twenty participants to create a conversational exchange. Based on those numbers, they knew how many subsequent meetings they should book and how many new accounts they should open. They had their sales funnel down to a science.

This worked well until the partner had an idea. "In the late 1990s, my partner said that if we wanted to have a modern, professional presentation that people took seriously, we should use overheads," the advisor said. "I agreed to go along, but a number of conditions had to be met."

The first was that they would carefully prepare their presentation and practice it until they were comfortable delivering it. Then, they would deliver it for an eight-week period, after which they would measure the results. They were surprised when they closed the loop and evaluated the impact on their sales funnel.

"Based on the number of people attending, bookings for face-to-face meetings dropped by twenty-five per cent during the eight weeks in question," he said. "As soon as we went back to the 'old' way of using a flip chart and simply talking to the audience, our numbers went back up."

The numbers stayed up until his partner had another idea. A few years later, he said that everyone was now using PowerPoint and that, to be taken seriously, they needed to change the way they delivered seminars.

The same conditions were imposed, but this time they practiced their presentation even more before unleashing it. The results were even more dramatic. "During the eight-week period that we used PowerPoint, our bookings for follow-up meetings dropped by fifty per cent," the advisor told me. "Again, when we went back to a simple approach of talking to people, those numbers went back up and have stayed up since."

This is not an isolated incident, by any means, and it underscores the sales opportunity that is available to those who have the courage to implement what we've talked about here. After examining the issue for more than twenty-five years, I am confident in saying that, regardless of whether your objective is to inform or persuade, fewer slides (if any at all) is the key to achieving the communication and business outcomes you're seeking.

The highest level of engagement is when the audience can confidently share your ideas with others after the presentation concludes. If people are talking about your ideas, and potentially defending your perspective, they are truly engaged. Your ideas have become part of who they are as human beings.

I once delivered a presentation in Washington, DC, to an international not-for-profit organization. I arrived when the previous series of presentations and breakout sessions were still in session. When the sessions ended and participants started grabbing coffee and snacks, I overheard a conversation among three colleagues.

One had been in the largest breakout room. When his colleagues asked about the presentation he attended, he positively gushed. "There are so many things the panelists talked about that we could use at our agency," he said, listing off a number of examples to support his point. "I'd love to stay and chat, but I'm going to find a quiet corner so I can go over my notes and think some more about how we can incorporate what they discussed. I want to share these with my team when we get back to the office."

And off he went. A few minutes later, I was refreshing my coffee when two panelists came out of the large breakout room. "How do you think our presentation went?" one asked the other.

"Not bad," was the reply. "But I really wish the moderator hadn't limited us to one slide each. I had a lot more information I wanted to show."

I had the opportunity to structure a client assignment that formalized the concept of sharing ideas with others while working with a mutual fund company that was preparing for a bi-annual sales conference. My role was to provide presentation training to investment managers, who would present to retail investment advisors at the conference. This was an extremely important sales opportunity for the firm. Investment advisors are its primary retail sales channel. They recommend investment options to retail clients. The goal is to have advisors confidently talk to clients about the investment approach of portfolio managers.

I worked with the investment managers to help them shape their stories and deliver presentations during breakout sessions. We wanted to create a conversational atmosphere that encouraged engagement, questions and dialogue. The assumption was that this would strengthen relationships, lead to more confidence among advisors in talking about the firm's investment options, and ultimately enhance sales.

The portfolio managers were divided into six presentation teams according to investment style. For about five weeks prior to the conference, each team participated in training and rehearsals.

Using the framework and a number of other tools in *The Presenter's Toolbox*, a resource available from most book sellers, I helped each presentation team shape its story to fill a forty-five-minute time frame (with half the time saved for questions). The remainder of the training focused on helping them deliver their investment stories effectively, while answering as many questions as possible and finishing within the forty-five minute time limit.

As the content development process unfolded, the breakout presentations became slide-free zones. This was not done by design, but it became clear to everyone that very few slides, if any, would be needed to tell each investment story effectively. As a result, projectors were removed from the breakout rooms, saving the company ten thousand dollars in rental fees.

And, instead of handing out a thick, cumbersome book of presentation slides at the conference (the previous conference provided a one hundred seventy-six-page full colour book of two slides per page that was likely never read), a short feature article (five to eight hundred words in length) was written to recap each presentation. A package of PDF articles was e-mailed to each advisor after the conference. The articles were easy to write once the portfolio team developed notes for their presentation. Each article simply became an extension of their notes. The logic was that investment advisors could share these articles in subsequent sales discussions with clients. The PDFs had embedded links to enable the company to track clicks to specific portions of its website.

Finally, the group established the objective of generating a Q-ratio equal of one or greater for each forty-five minute presentation. Presenters strove to answer more than forty-five questions each, while completing their presentation content and finishing on time.

The approach was exceptionally effective. Each breakout session generated fifty to eighty questions from advisors, exceeding a Q-ratio of one. The audience was fully engaged. Some of the comments on evaluations included:

- Very interactive, especially amongst the fund managers. Hope to see this more often at future conferences.

- Outstanding in every sense.

- Great interaction during the conference.

- Interactive and informative. Very enjoyable.

- The best conference of its kind that I've ever attended.

All speakers achieved a rating equal to or greater than four out of five on evaluations, with a median grade of four-point-three. To put this into perspective, the final professional keynote speaker (Michael Lewis of *Moneyball* fame), achieved a rating of four-point-five.

In addition, ninety-six per cent of attendees rated the investment teams as industry-leading or strong. Seventy-one per cent of attendees said they would be more willing to recommend this company's investment products to their clients. Seventy-seven per cent said they would make this mutual fund company one of the top three mutual fund companies they recommend to their clients.

And the sales results have since spoken for themselves.

Engagement is as engagement does. People do not engage with slides. They engage with other human beings who have something of value to share, and share it in an engaging way.

Engage the audience. Ensure that they think about your ideas. Allow them to probe and question. Give them the opportunity to turn your ideas into their ideas. By doing so, your ability to inform, educate, influence and persuade will be considerably enhanced, regardless of whether you're talking to one person or thousands.

ONE FINAL DROP

The promise of the modern age is the ability to create conversations that never before existed. We can text. We can tweet. We can exchange information on social media. We can participate in video calls on our tablets or smartphones.

At their core, conversations are back-and-forth exchanges. You send a short piece of information and you get something back, even if only in the form of a nod while you're talking to someone in person, an "uh-huh" over the telephone, or an "lol" during a text exchange. It's like a game of tennis. The ball goes from one side to the other and back again in a two-way process that keeps both sides engaged.

Most presentations today are like playing tennis with someone who has a large basket of balls and isn't going to stop serving until the basket is empty, regardless of whether you show any interest in hitting one back. In such situations, if you came to practice service returns, you might be interested in playing along. But if you came to play a game of tennis, it won't take long before you find something else to do.

I had a discussion once with a workshop participant that highlighted the difference between a basket of balls approach versus a back-and-forth exchange, and the reaction of audiences to each. The participant told me she had conducted a customer seminar and invited two speakers, an accountant and a lawyer. In her mind, the accountant did everything right. He showed up early, ensured the projector was working and delivered his presentation. He presented a lot of information that she felt was incredibly valuable, although she admitted as we talked that, while the information was very familiar to her, it was less familiar to those in attendance. The accountant ran a few minutes over his allotted time because he answered questions at the end of his presentation.

When it was his turn to speak, the lawyer pulled his chair to the front of the room, turned off the projector, sat down, and started talking. At one point, he brought over another chair and draped his arm over the back of it.

"He was slouching," she said. At the time, she was offended that the lawyer didn't take the seminar seriously enough to sit up straight. But he was being himself.

The lawyer referred to the accountant's presentation a few times, which led her to believe that the lawyer didn't take time to prepare a presentation (and led me to think that the accountant had prepared more than enough information for two presentations). People were encouraged to share their particular situation in general terms for the benefit of the group, and to ask questions throughout. The lawyer had an extended conversation with those in attendance.

At the end of the evening, the results of the evaluation forms shocked her. "The lawyer scored so much higher than the accountant," she told me. "At the time, I couldn't believe it. He wasn't prepared. He didn't bring a single slide. He slouched. He broke every rule in the standard presentation skills book.

"But after attending your workshop, I now understand. He didn't present. He conversed. He invited the audience's perspective and answered their questions. Participants got more value from the back-and-forth exchange than from the presentation that preceded it."

I said at the beginning of this book that you have a choice. You can choose to deliver your presentations one slide at a time. Or you can apply what we've talked about here, and deliver your ideas one bucket at a time.

However, there really isn't a choice if your goal is to communicate effectively. If you wish to have more of your ideas understood, remembered, applied, acted upon and discussed intelligently with others, the science is clear. Even the skimpiest of written information that's shown while someone is talking overloads working memory. The audience cannot think and listen at the same time. They cannot read and listen at the same time. And they most assuredly cannot read and think and listen at the same time.

Structuring your ideas and delivering them conversationally is the best possible way to have those ideas travel from you to them. By creating equal, engaging partnerships with audiences, I have no doubt that you'll improve your ability to inform, educate, influence and persuade any audience important to your personal or professional success.

All it takes is the courage to make the right choice, and the willingness to use the insights here and in *The Presenter's Toolbox* to proceed accordingly.

The Author

Eric first became fascinated with the power of the spoken word in 1981. The professor of his college presentation course was leading a team that was preparing a presentation for delivery in Baden-Baden, (West) Germany. The purpose of the presentation was to convince the International Olympic Committee to select Calgary as host of the 1988 Olympic Winter Games.

"We were given a peek inside the strategic process," Eric recalls. "I'll never forget the moment I heard the news that Calgary had been selected to host the games. It was a defining moment of my career. I was hooked on the power of the spoken word."

Eric started his communications career as a government public affairs officer in June, 1982, and wrote his first speech for a senior government executive less than a year later. "It was a retirement speech, so it was fairly low risk," he says. "But I worked almost five hours to craft that five minutes. I received a lovely note from the speaker, which I still have."

He left government in September, 1985, and set out on his own as a freelance communication consultant. For the first eight to ten years of his freelance career, he wrote hundreds of speeches for executives in the private, public and not-for-profit sectors, earning local, national and international awards for his work.

In the 1990s, he began providing presentation skills training and one-on-one coaching. Over a span of thirty-plus years, he has helped thousands of clients from six continents develop effective, compelling, meaningful content for a host of speaking challenges. He has helped them deliver that content memorably with a conversational style, one bucket at a time.

Eric holds a bachelor of arts in communication studies and a two-year college diploma in advertising and public relations. He received designations as an accredited business communicator (ABC) in 1991 and an accredited public relations practitioner (APR) in 1993. In 2002, he was named a master communicator (MC), which is the highest distinction that can be bestowed on a Canadian member of the International Association of Business Communicators. In 2015, he joined the College of Fellows of the Canadian Public Relations Society.

Presentation content that almost develops itself

The Presenter's Toolbox provides an excellent alternative to using slideware like Power-Point or Keynote to develop content for any type of speech, lecture or presentation.

The Presenter's Toolbox will help you shape your strategy and develop clear, compelling content. You'll shift your re-sources—your time—from spending hours mucking around with slides to focusing on audience needs and strengthening your strategic focus. As you work through the tools, you'll discover that your content almost develops itself.

And because you'll almost certainly use fewer slides during your presentations, you'll increase the chances of achieving your personal, professional and business objectives.

By using *The Toolbox*, you will save time. Your content will be meaningful to the audience, which enhances your chances of being memorable.

The Presenter's Toolbox is available online from most book sellers.

Made in the USA
Middletown, DE
20 November 2020